Restoring Upholstered Furniture

Restoring Upholstered Furniture

Lorrie Mack with Geoffrey Hayley

Drawings by Wendy Jones

Orbis · London

Dedication
To Daddy

Acknowledgments

The author is grateful to the following:
Tristram Holland, Sarah Chapman, Wendy Jones,
Paul Welti, Kit Johnson, Jean Morley, and
especially to Geoff and Ken Hayley and their
staff at Satoll, including Wah, Louise, John,
Albert and Jean.

The publishers are grateful to the following for
permission to reproduce the photographs in this
book:
Oranje-Nassau Museum, Delft: 6; Jonathan
Bourne: 8; M. H. Bedford: 102; B. I. Bury:
103 (all); Elizabeth Whiting: 110.

Other photographs were specially taken for the
book by Paul Williams, Michael Plomer, Jon
Bouchier and David Johnson.

Fabric for padded wicker armchair by Sanderson.

Printed in Italy by IGDA, Novara

ISBN 0-85613-714-6

Contents

Introduction

The term 'upholstery' covers virtually every kind of covered seating, from a single thickness of material laid over a hard, rough surface to a fully sprung and elaborately padded sofa. The amount of work involved in restoring an upholstered piece of furniture is dictated by its original structure, and this can range from a simple padded seat without springs to a large chesterfield with scroll arms and deep buttoning.

Fashions in furniture have changed often and dramatically over the years and there are many possible permutations of shape, structure and decoration to be seen. We have tried to include as many of these as possible in the projects in this book, but you may find it necessary to use the instructions given for the seat of one chair, the arms of another and the back of a third for the particular piece you are restoring.

It is very important that you tackle two or three of the smaller projects which contain basic techniques like attaching webbing, lashing springs and applying padding before you go on to the larger, more complex ones. Read the

The invention of the coil spring encouraged the fashion for overstuffed buttoned furniture.

In the 1880s the popular daybed, or divan, was embellished with richly patterned coverings and plenty of buttons, fringes and tassels.

glossary before you begin, to familiarize yourself with the terms, then look through your chosen project and examine the drawings to get an overall picture of its structure. Work slowly and carefully and be absolutely sure that each stage is done properly before you move on to the next, since every layer is built on the previous one. Upholstery is not a simple diversion to fill the odd afternoon; it is a complicated undertaking requiring hard work, but makes a very rewarding hobby.

We have given instructions for complete reupholstering in all our projects, but your furniture may need only a little renewing. Tacking on a layer of webbing directly over the old one, and adding a little extra stuffing and a fresh new cover may be all that's required.

You can save money by reusing the old springs (if they are straight and firm) and by replacing some of the covering fabric with pieces of hessian or other fabric where it won't show, for example for the sections which pull to the rails for tacking and the area under the cushion.

Your work will be easier if you raise it off the ground to a comfortable height. A table top is slightly too high but will do at a pinch. If you are planning to do a lot of upholstery, you should invest in a pair of low trestles.

We have tried to make each section completely self-contained and easy to follow, so that the techniques shown and explained will give you the confidence to start each project and the skill necessary to finish it.

The development of upholstery

Upholstery as we know it today did not really come into being until the coil spring was invented in 1828. Before then, the important influences on furniture design mainly affected the shape, construction and ornamentation of wood rather than upholstery, and for hundreds of years seating was a convenience rather than an aid to relaxation.

In medieval times, if you sat at all, it was usually on a kind of low wooden or stone ledge attached to the inside wall of the house, insulated perhaps with a rug or skin draped over it. There were several reasons for this seating arrangement: no

Introduction

one could attack you from behind, no small concern in those days; and if danger threatened in the form of an army or disease, a household had to be able to move on immediately, and so cumbersome pieces of furniture had no place.

Early free-standing furniture retained a bench-like construction, which developed into the earliest version of what we know as a settle, while the first free-standing seating for one person was the stool. It was found that a three-legged seat would stand firm on uneven surfaces, while a stool with four legs would not. Many stools had a slung leather seat which was more flexible and thus more comfortable than a rigid wooden one. Later, more sophisticated one-person seats with a back and arms came into use, but they were strictly for the head of the household or important guests, and until the end of the fifteenth century proper chairs were a rarity. Many had an 'X' construction so they could be folded up and carried easily from place to place (a shape

This Hepplewhite chair of 1788 shows how upholstery was still secondary to an intricately carved frame at this period.

which survived even when portability was no longer a requirement and the chairs became very heavy and richly ornamented). Even though the ornamentation of seating increased, chairs remained straight and hard, the first concession to the human form being merely a more gentle slope to the chair back.

Early attempts at upholstery involved putting some sort of pad on the hard seat, of horsehair or fur or, if these materials were not available, moss; but it was not until the end of the sixteenth century that padding began to be attached to the frame permanently, first to seats only, then to the backs and arms of chairs. A widely held and quite sensible theory is that this only started to happen when heavily padded clothing — especially for men — went out of fashion and the discomfort of rigid seats could be felt for the first time.

With faster methods of weaving cloth, the demand for more comfortable and elaborate furniture brought about by increased wealth and social stability could be met. Seats and backs were richly ornamented and padded with wool, hair or pieces of scrap fabric covered with sumptuous materials such as velvet or brocade. The new technique of fixed padding was soon extended to the settle, which, by 1700, had been transformed into the settee. At about the same time the daybed came into common use; this was another type of long seat but it had no back and only one end which was either fixed or adjustable.

The eighteenth century was a period when the concepts of beauty and function came together in furniture design. Formal society became increasingly important and leisure was taken very seriously, resulting in the design and production of suitable chairs in which to read, play cards, serve tea or exchange news and opinions. Buttoning, developed for padding coaches to protect the occupants from the bumps in the appalling roads of the time, was extended to domestic seating, where it has been used, to a greater or lesser degree, ever since. Still, no chair allowed its user to relax completely. The frame was still of paramount importance and the architectural and design fashions of the eighteenth century — curly rococo, bizarre chinoiserie, restrained neo-classicism and delicate Sheraton — were reflected here rather than in upholstery.

The Regency period (1800–30) saw a return to the styles of the Ancient World, and fashions in furniture as well as in architecture and clothing

Fluting, used in various ways on these items from a catalogue, was a very popular form of ornamentation in the early nineteenth century. Note the buttoning on the sleigh.

reflected this. Although sofas and daybeds had been in use for some time, it was not common for people actually to lie on them unless they were old or ill, but the early nineteenth century found fashionable people lolling about on all manner of sofas, single-ended daybeds and Ottomans, which had no back or arms at all.

Through all these changes in style and usage, the basic structure of upholstery remained the same: padding was provided by layers of fabric, wool or horsehair. It was not until the advent of the coiled spring, with its ability to retain its resilience almost indefinitely, that the look, feel and function of seating changed dramatically, and a chair's padding became its most important feature. The typically overstuffed look of Victorian furniture, with its huge proportions, elaborate buttoning, deep springing on seat, back and arms, and richly ornamented covering fabric, may seem ugly to us today, but it was during this heyday of highly upholstered seating that the techniques of modern upholstery were fully developed. Even though the use of foam dominates the manufacture of mass-produced furniture today, these techniques are still in use, almost unchanged, for traditional furniture upholstered by hand.

Terms, tools and materials

anchor (twine or cord)
to drive a tack into the frame a short distance, slip a looped length of twine round the tack, then drive the tack home.

back-tacking
method of attaching outer covers which hides the tacks used; also refers to the strip 13 mm ($\frac{1}{2}$ in) wide used in this process (available in rolls). You can also use a strip of any stiff card for the purpose.

bias
diagonal direction across fabric. Cutting cloth in this way makes it slightly stretchy so it can more easily be manipulated round curves.

blanket stitch
looped stitch used for edging or to join two folded edges of fabric.

blind (sink) stitch
edge stitch made with twine on scrim-covered hair or ginger fibre and forming a loop inside the padding to consolidate it.

bridle ties
loops of twine which hold padding (hair or fibre) in place.

calico (muslin)
plain unbleached cotton sometimes used as a final cover for the padding before the covering fabric is put on.

cane
bamboo cane 25 mm (1 in) thick bent into a broad U shape and used to support the front of an upholstered seat.

chamfer (bevel)
to file down a right-angled corner to make a flat, angled surface.

Courtelle
thin bonded polyester material, used as a final padding underneath the covering fabric.

Dacron
thick bonded polyester covered by a sheet of cheesecloth and used to wrap a central core of foam for cushions.

double bayonet needle
straight needle with a spear-shaped point at both ends, used for stitching rolls, anchoring stuffing and other jobs which are too heavy for a plain straight needle.

drive home
to hammer a tack in as far as it will go, making a permanent anchor.

facing
shaped, fabric-covered piece of plywood applied to the front of a scroll arm to give a neat appearance and conceal the tacks on the front of the arm.

file
metal instrument with roughened surface used for shaping or smoothing wood.

foam
dense plastic or rubber material, available in different qualities and used for seats, for back and arm padding and for cushions.

gimp
narrow tape, available in a wide variety of colours, which is used to cover tacks and raw edges. Gimp is more expensive than ordinary braid because it is woven in such a way that it can go smoothly and flatly around curves and awkward corners.

gimp pin
thin tack with a tiny head used to attach gimp (q.v.) or braid. Usually available in a large range of colours.

ginger fibre (coir fibre)
long, coarse fibres which come from the inside of the coconut husk; used as the first layer of stuffing over springs.

grain
the lines of fibres in wood or fabric.

hammer
see under magnetic hammer.

hessian (burlap)
woven jute material used for separating different upholstery layers and especially for covering springs. Available in several different weights, although 340 g (12 oz) is the most commonly used.

horsehair (curled hair)
usually, in fact, a mixture of hair from horses, cattle and pigs, twisted and heated to a high temperature to sterilize it and set the curl. It is the softest and springiest stuffing and, since it is very expensive, used most often for the top layer of padding only.

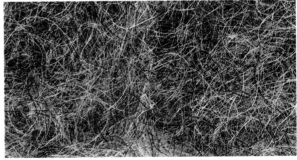

lashing (cording)
process by which springs are tied to each other and attached to the frame so they remain stable in use.

11

Terms, tools and materials

linter felt
soft, thick, coarse felted cotton, used as one of the final layers of padding.

magnetic hammer
upholsterer's hammer with a two-pronged claw and a magnetic head to pick up tacks. This is an optional piece of equipment, and a non-magnetized hammer will do just as well, as long as it has a fairly small head so that the wood surrounding each tack is not damaged.

mallet
wooden cabinet-maker's tool used to tap the head of a chisel when removing tacks.

panel pin
thin, headless tack used to fix a fabric-covered piece of wood such as a facing (q.v.). It is driven straight through the fabric, which is then eased over it so it becomes invisible.

piping cord
twisted cord, usually made of cotton. Covered with a strip of fabric, it is used as a trim to give a neat finish to final covers. (Wash and dry piping cord before you use it, to shrink it.)

rasp
coarser version of a file (q.v.).

regulator needle
a flat-ended needle used to arrange, or 'regulate', the stuffing inside its cover. The flat end is used to tuck fabric into narrow places and for buttoning.

ripping chisel
flat-ended tool, similar to a screwdriver, used with a mallet for removing tacks.

rubberized hair
horsehair (curled hair) bonded with latex rubber and then compressed.

running stitch
simple in-and-out stitch used for tacking and for anchoring layers of padding.

scrim
a loosely woven version of hessian, also made of jute, used to cover the first layer of stuffing before the edges are stitched.

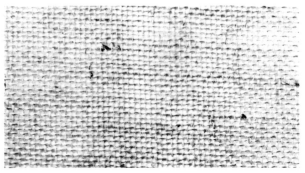

selvedge
side edge of fabric, woven very densely so that it cannot unravel.

skewers
straight pins with a looped end, used for anchoring materials in place temporarily.

sheet or skin wadding
compressed cotton fibres on a thin 'skin' of cotton which holds them together. Used, skin side up, to prevent padding — horsehair or fibre — from working through the covering fabric.

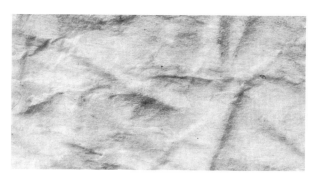

slip knot
simple and very common upholstery knot used for fixing springs, for buttoning, and for starting off a line of stitching.

slip stitch
nearly invisible stitch used most often to attach the piped sections of covering fabric to each other or to sew up the opening left in a cushion cover for the pad to be inserted.

slipping needle
small half-circle needle used for slip-stitching.

slipping (buttoning) thread
strong, fine twine or thread suitable for buttoning.

springing needle
large, curved needle used for attaching springs and sewing through stuffing. (Larger and stronger than a half-circle needle.)

springs
double-cone springs of different sizes and gauges (metal diameter) are used in the projects in this book. Their coils diminish in size towards their centre, or 'waist'.

staples
are a much easier and quicker way than tacks of fixing layers of material to the frame of a piece of furniture. Since, however, almost all frames are made of hard wood, a hand-operated staple gun will not exert enough pressure to drive the staples in, so you will have to invest in an electric or compressed air model if you want to avoid tacking. These are very expensive, but worthwhile for doing a lot of upholstery work.

straight grain
direction of fabric weave, either parallel to the selvedge or at right angles to it.

straight needle
slim, double-pointed stitching needle used mainly for buttoning.

tack or tape roll
highly compressed roll of foam which is tacked to the frame to replace back- and top-stitched edge rolls.

tacks
small-headed nails used to hold upholstery in place. They come in two main types: 'improved' which are fairly thick with a largish head, and 'fine', which are thinner with a smaller head. Within these types, tacks are available in various sizes. Remember that the tack chosen must provide a suitably strong anchor without splitting the wood.

Tailor's tacks
temporary stitches used in upholstery mainly to mark the positioning of buttoning on fabric.

template
piece of paper, card or thin wood used as a pattern for cutting out a section of fabric, or the front facings for scroll arms.

temporary tack
tack driven in only a short way so it can be removed and the material it is anchoring readjusted.

top stitch
edge stitch formed with twine (q.v.) on scrim-covered hair or fibre in order to make a firm roll, separate from the main padded area.

trestles
large, A-shaped wooden supports which can be used to raise a piece of furniture to a comfortable working height. They could be a useful investment if you were going to be doing a lot of upholstery; otherwise, a large sturdy table will do.

twine
strong, waxed fine twist made from flax and hemp or sometimes from various synthetic materials. All the twine used in this book is No. 2 upholsterer's twine.

upholsterer's linen
closely woven black cloth used to make the cover for the base, or 'bottoming', of a piece of upholstered furniture.

webbing
strips of woven material usually 50 mm (2 in) wide, used to support the entire upholstered structure. We have used 'black and white' webbing (made from flax and cotton) throughout because it is the best quality, but jute can also be used.

webbing stretcher
handled wooden tool used for stretching webbing over a frame. The one used in this book is called a 'bat' stretcher, and you can easily make one yourself by cutting a hole the width of your webbing in a rectangular block of wood and making a peg from a length of dowelling, attached to the wood with a cord. Shape one end of the wood into a handle for a comfortable grip. Alternatively, use a simple block of wood with a right-angled groove cut in it to pull webbing taut.

13

Project 1
Padded wicker armchair

Introduction

This project — padding a pretty, old-fashioned wicker chair — introduces some of the basic techniques of upholstery and also calls for simple sewing skills. The methods used will result in padding with much of the comfort of traditional upholstery for a great deal less cost and effort.

The structure of the upholstery is simple: the back and sides are made up as a single piece, consisting of a layer of soft stuffing (Courtelle) sandwiched between two pieces of fabric (one of which will be visible through the woven wicker) and held together with buttons which also add visual interest. The seat padding is a thick, piped cushion which, like the back, is removable.

You will find the work easier and the result more attractive if you choose a plain fabric or one without a very large pattern.

Tools

scissors

pencil

tape-measure or ruler

pins

sewing machine

75 mm (3 in) springing or half-circle needle (a large, straight one will do)

250 mm (10 in) double bayonet needle (or a large darning needle)

tailor's chalk

upholstery or kitchen skewers — about six

small slipping needle

Materials

pieces of brown paper or newsprint large enough to cover the seat and go round the back and sides of your chair, to make templates

sticky tape

covering fabric: when you have cut out all the templates, use them to calculate the amount of fabric you will need, allowing for any centred pattern or pattern repeat, and adding extra for piping, seat cushion borders, buttons and tabs for tying the back padding to the chair. (Our chair took approximately 4 m ($4\frac{1}{2}$ yd) of fabric.)

115 g (4 oz) Courtelle: measure the height and width of the chair back and sides and buy twice this amount (or four times if you can get only 60 g (2 oz) Courtelle)

kit for making fabric-covered buttons: the number of buttons you need and their size will depend on the size of your chair and the pattern — if any — of your fabric. (We used ten pairs.)

piping cord — specify $\frac{3}{8}$ or $1\frac{1}{2}$ — enough to go twice round the seat template

seating foam 75 mm (3 in) thick, or 90 mm ($3\frac{1}{2}$ in) if Dacron is not being used

510 g (18 oz) Dacron — enough to wrap round the seating foam (optional)

slipping or button thread and cotton to match fabric

matching zip long enough to go round the curve at the back of the cushion and allow the seat pad to be inserted. (Ours was 610 mm (24 in) long.)

Project 1

Figures 1–15 The back and arms

Figures 1 & 2 Making the template

Cut a piece of brown paper or newsprint large enough to cover the inside arms and back of your chair. Alternatively, you may find it easier to use one piece of paper for the back and one for each side, taping the three pieces together firmly. Place the paper in position, shape it to the chair as accurately as possible, and tape it round the frame. You may find this easier if you slit the edges of the paper where it goes over the outer curves of the chair (but make sure these slits do not go into the paper where it covers the area to be padded) (1).

Smoothing the paper flat against the chair, pencil in the outline of where the padding will fit, and draw lines to divide the back section from each side section. Check the fit repeatedly as you go. Remove the paper from the chair and cut carefully along the pencil lines to make three pieces which, when butted together and joined with tape, make a template of exactly the same size and shape as the finished pad will be (2). Fit the finished template to your chair, smooth it into the curves and make any small adjustments that may be necessary.

When you are satisfied that your template fits the chair as accurately as possible, cut and separate the back and arm sections again so that you have three pieces of paper from which to cut your fabric. It may seem as though this cutting, taping and cutting again is wasted effort, but if you check and alter where necessary at each of these stages it will make your pattern far more accurate, and you will avoid mistakes later when you cut out the fabric. If the paper becomes creased or crumpled, smooth it out with a cool iron.

Figure 3 Cutting out the fabric

Lay your fabric out flat, right side up. Making sure that any pattern runs in the right direction, place the back template on the fabric so that an imaginary central line along its length would be parallel with the straight grain. Pin the template to the fabric and, leaving a seam allowance of 40 mm (1½ in), cut round it. Turn the template over and cut round it again (leaving a seam allowance) to make the outside back cover of the pad, matching the pattern to that on the front if you wish (3).

Figure 1

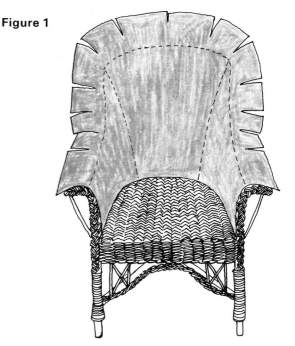

Figure 2

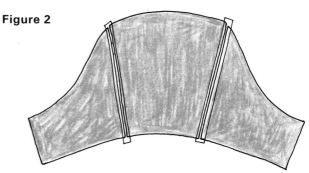

Figure 3

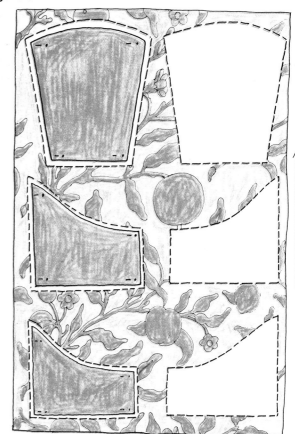

Repeat the process with the arm templates, making sure that the pattern runs in the same direction as that on the back pieces, as on the suggested cutting layout (figure 3).

Figure 4 Making up the cover

With the right sides of the fabric together, pin each pair of arm pieces to one of the back pieces. Machine-sew the four seams and press them flat. With right sides together, pin the inside and outside covers to each other, and then sew up the sides and across the top, but leave the bottom open (**4**). Turn this 'bag' right side out.

Figures 5 & 6 Padding the cover

Fold the 115 g (4 oz) Courtelle in half to make a double thickness. Place the cover on top of it and cut round it but about 25 mm (1 in) outside it so that the Courtelle is the same shape as the cover but larger (**5**).

Thread a 75 mm (3 in) needle with a piece of slipping thread (or button thread) about 2 m (78 in) long. Using blanket stitch, sew round the outside of the two layers of Courtelle to join them together neatly. Insert the Courtelle into the case, working it into the corners and edges with your fingers to give a soft, plumped effect.

Starting at the centre of the open edge of the cover, turn in a small hem towards the Courtelle on both sides of the fabric, pin the sides together and slip-stitch along this edge to both ends of the opening (**6**), to enclose the padding completely.

Figures 7–12 Buttoning the back and arms

The purpose of buttoning is to hold the fabric and the padding firmly together.

With the padded cover laid flat on a table in front of you, work out the number of buttons you will need: to do this you should place them approximately 150 mm (6 in) apart and a little less in from the top edge. Mark the position of the buttons with pins (**7**), and make up a pair of covered buttons from the kit for each point you have marked.

Figure 4

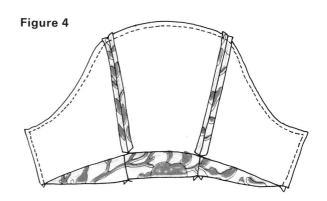

Figure 5

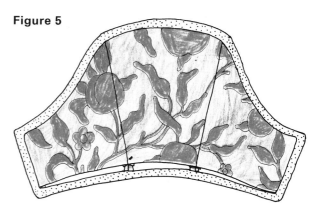

Figure 6

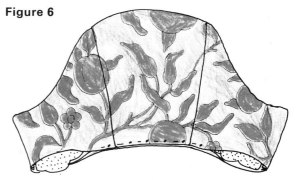

Figure 7

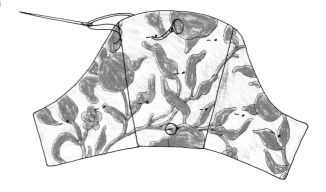

17

Project 1

Thread the shank of one button on to about 1 m (40 in) of twine. Now thread both ends of the twine through the eye of a 250 mm (10 in) double bayonet needle (or a large darning needle) and push the needle through the padded cover from front to back (**8**). Turn the pad over and thread one end of the twine through the shank of another button (**9**). Remove the needle, make a slip knot (**10** and **12**) and pull tightly. Trim the twine under the button (**11**). Repeat the process until all the buttons are attached.

Figures 13-15 Making and attaching the tabs

On the straight grain of the remaining fabric, cut out four strips measuring 75 mm x 600 mm (3 in x 24 in). Fold each strip in half lengthways, right sides together, and machine-stitch 10 mm ($\frac{3}{8}$ in) in from the raw edges, leaving a gap in the centre so that you can turn the tab right side out easily (**13**). Turn right side out (**14**) and press.

Pin the centres of the four tabs to the top edge of the back of the cover at the points shown (**15**), the ones at each end placed about 40 mm ($1\frac{1}{2}$ in) diagonally in from the corners. Stitch the tabs securely to the cover in a straight line across the centre of each tab.

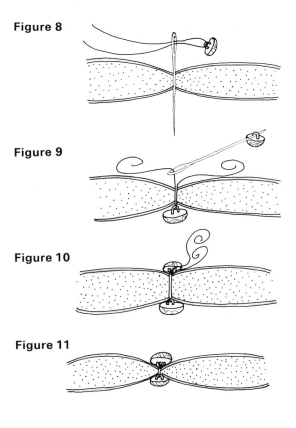

Figure 8

Figure 9

Figure 10

Figure 11

Figure 12

Figure 13

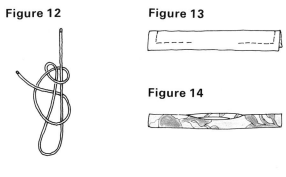

Figure 14

Figure 15

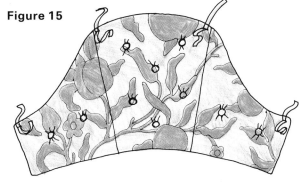

The wicker chair shown on page 15, before it was upholstered.

Figures 16–32 The seat

Figures 16 & 17 Cutting out the seat pad cover

To make a template for the seat pad cover, first draw a shape on paper to the measurements of the seat and cut this out. Tie the padded back cover in place, then lay the paper on the chair seat and mark out the curves with a pencil. Cut just outside this line, then replace it on the seat and trim again if necessary to ensure an accurate fit.

Pin the template to the right side of the fabric, centring the pattern and with the central line of the template parallel to the straight grain. Cut round it, leaving a 13 mm ($\frac{1}{2}$ in) seam allowance (**16**). Turn the template over and cut out a second piece of fabric the same size for the underside of the cover. (Keep the template for cutting out the seat pad itself.)

To make the border for the cover, measure the three straight sides of the template, add 25 mm (1 in) for two seam allowances, and cut a 115 mm ($4\frac{1}{2}$ in)-wide strip of fabric of this length at right angles to the selvedge. With right sides together, pin this strip to the three straight sides of one of the seat sections (the zip will be on the curved side). Now measure the curved end of the template (the length of your zip) and, again adding 25 mm (1 in) to this measurement for the seams, cut out two more strips of fabric but make them each 75 mm (3 in) wide. Check their fit by pinning them in position on the seat section (**17**).

Figures 18 & 19 Inserting the zip

Along one long edge of one of the 75 mm (3 in) strips, turn under a 20 mm ($\frac{3}{4}$ in) hem so that the wrong sides of the fabric are facing each other. Place the folded edge along the centre of the zip. Machine-stitch the zip to the fabric (**18**); then attach the other narrow fabric strip to the other side of the zip in the same way (**19**), so that the teeth of the zip are hidden. Fold this zip panel in half crossways and cut a small nick in the fabric at the fold on both edges (figure 19).

Figure 20 Fitting the border

Fold the top and bottom seat sections in half lengthways and make a small nick in the edge of the fabric at each of the central points. With right sides together, pin the zip panel to the curved edge of one section, matching nicks.

Figure 16

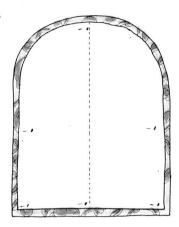

Figure 17

Figure 18

Figure 19

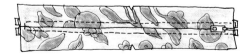

Project 1

Now pin the main border strip round the rest of the seat section, centring it on the second nick, and pin it to the zip panel. Trim to fit if necessary, and machine-stitch the border strip to the zip panel with two 13 mm ($\frac{1}{2}$ in) seams (**20**). Machine-stitch over both ends of the zip several times, to strengthen it.

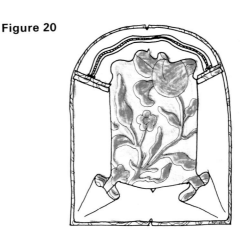
Figure 20

Figures 21–25 Preparing the piping

The purpose of piping on upholstered furniture is to provide a neat, attractive finish and to strengthen the seams. Fabric for piping is always cut into strips diagonally (on the bias) so that it will 'give' and enable the resulting piping to be eased round corners smoothly.

Cut enough bias strips (**21**) 40–50 mm (1$\frac{1}{2}$–2 in) wide so that, joined together, they will go easily round the perimeter of the cushion cover twice.

Trim off any selvedges and join the strips, right sides together and leaving a 6 mm ($\frac{1}{4}$ in) seam, so that they will be straight when the seam is opened (**22**). Join all the strips together in this way. Press the seams open and trim (**23**).

Lay the piping cord down the centre of the wrong side of the bias strip, starting 13 mm ($\frac{1}{2}$ in) in from the end (**24**). Make a small nick in each side of the fabric at this point, and fold the fabric over the cord. Pin and baste the fabric as close to the cord as possible, then, using a piping or zipper foot, machine-stitch along the edge of the cord, starting 50 mm (2 in) from the end (**25**).

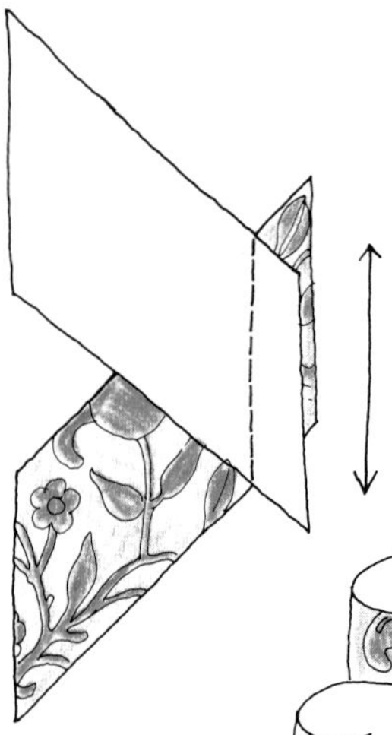

Figures 26–29 Attaching the piping to the border

Matching the nicks in the end of your piping to those in the centre of the zip panel, pin the piping strip to one side of the panel, right sides and raw edges together (**26**). Starting where the stitching begins on the piping, machine-stitch as closely as possible to the cord, on top of the existing line of stitching.

Sew round the whole border, stopping 50 mm (2 in) before the starting point. Make a nick in the end you are working with to coincide with the nick in the border. Cut the piping off 6 mm ($\frac{1}{4}$ in) past this nick (**27**). Pick up the two loose ends of bias fabric, place them right sides together so that the nicks are matching (**28**), and sew them together. Press this seam open and trim the cords so that they butt against each other. Fold the fabric back over the piping and stitch the remaining gap in the seam between the piping and the border (**29**).

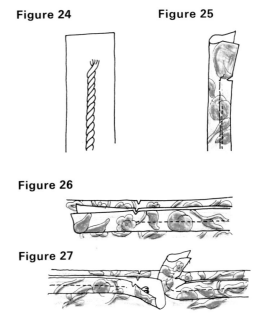

Figure 21

Figure 22

Figure 23

Figure 24

Figure 25

Figure 26

Figure 27

Measure 90 mm (3½ in) from the edge of the piping across the border strip to determine the position of the second strip of piping. Mark this measurement with tailor's chalk all round the border. Using the mark as a guide, sew on the second piping strip in the same way as the first.

Figure 28

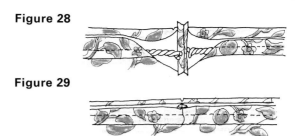

Figure 29

Figure 30 Finishing the seat pad cover

Matching the nicks on the zip panel and the curved edge of one of the seat sections, and with right sides and raw edges together, pin the border to the seat section and machine-sew on top of the existing stitching. Clip into the seam allowance of the piping strip and border, at the curves and almost to the stitching line at the corners, to allow for ease of fitting (**30**).

Figure 30

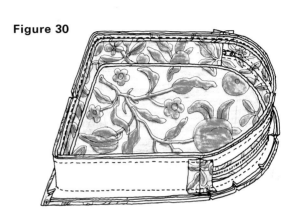

Sew another row of stitching 3 mm (⅛ in) outside the first row all round, to reinforce the seam. Trim the seam allowance to within 6 mm (¼ in) of this second row of stitching.

Join the second seat section to the border in the same way as the first, making sure that the zip is open before you do this so that you can turn the cushion cover right side out. Turn and press.

Figures 31 & 32 Making the seat pad

The following instructions are for a foam pad wrapped in a soft, thick layer of Dacron, but you can have the seat pad simply made of thicker foam and insert it directly into the cover.

Figure 31

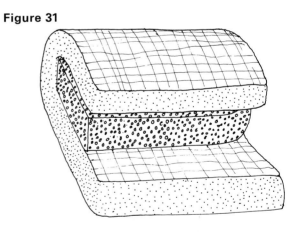

You will need a foam pad 75 mm (3 in) thick and exactly the same area as the seat template. Ask the retailer which type of foam is most suitable and take your template to the shop so they can cut the foam for you.

Take a piece of 510 g (18 oz) Dacron large enough to wrap right round the foam pad from side to side (**31**). Pin the ends and sides together through the covering net with upholstery (or kitchen) skewers. Trim off any excess fibre round the edges, leaving the covering net for sewing together (see figure 32). With a small slipping needle and slipping thread, use large blanket stitches to sew the edges of the netting together (**32**). Fold the netting neatly at the corners to make a square shape.

Figure 32

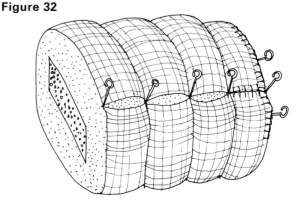

Ease the finished pad into the cushion cover, pushing it carefully into place so it feels smooth and soft and fits neatly at the corners. Zip up the cover, taking care not to catch the netting in the zip.

Project 2
Chair with drop-in seat

Introduction

This type of chair (usually a dining chair) has a separate seat which consists of a simple wooden frame covered with padding which is supported by strips of webbing. The seat can be lifted out of the chair frame, repaired and then replaced; a few small dowels or screws may hold it in place, but once these are taken out, it should come free with a light tap from underneath with a hammer or mallet.

There are two important techniques, described for the first time in this project, which will be featured in almost every piece of upholstery you come across: attaching strips of webbing which support the whole structure; and making bridle ties which hold the horsehair or fibre padding in place.

Unless you are simply changing the outer covering, you will almost certainly need to strip the seat right down to its frame in order to reupholster it, since broken or sagging webbing is usually the main cause of any problem.

Tools

mallet
ripping chisel
tape-measure
chalk or pencil
scissors or sharp knife
webbing stretcher
hammer
springing needle
regulator needle (or large bradawl)

Materials

black and white (first-quality) webbing — see figure 3 for measurements and add 500 mm (20 in)
20 mm ($\frac{5}{8}$ in) improved tacks
280 or 340 g (10 or 12 oz) hessian — one piece slightly larger than the seat frame
13 mm ($\frac{1}{2}$ in) fine tacks
twine (upholsterer's twine is always sold by the reel)
horsehair — gauge approximately how much you need from the old stuffing
calico — approximately 1 m (1 yd)
10 mm ($\frac{3}{8}$ in) fine tacks
sheet (skin) wadding — enough to cover the top of your seat
60 g (2 oz) Courtelle — one piece slightly larger than your seat
covering fabric — enough to go over the top of the seat to the underside of the frame
black upholstery linen or hessian — 0·5 m ($\frac{1}{2}$ yd)

Project 2

Figures 1 & 2 Removing the old upholstery

As you remove the old upholstery, note how the different layers have been attached. Although it is extremely unlikely that you will be able to reuse any of the materials except the horsehair, you should keep them to estimate quantities.

Turn the seat upside-down and, with a mallet and ripping chisel, remove the tacks attaching the hessian which covers the underside of the seat frame, working carefully in the direction of the wood's grain and making sure that the edge of the chisel slides under the tacks. In the same way, remove the tacks holding the top, decorative covering fabric which should also be attached to the underside of the seat frame; keep this as a pattern from which to cut your new cover. If you find another cover just below it, untack it in the same way. Turn the seat over and remove these covers and the layer of sheet (skin) wadding just below them. You should now find a piece of calico, again tacked to the underside of the frame: remove the tacks in the same way as before and take it off. Under this layer is a horsehair pad fastened down with twine. Cut the twine and remove the pad. (You may be able to reuse this pad: if it is in good condition but very flat, tease the fibres until you have a thick, loose mass.)

Under the pad is a layer of hessian tacked on to the frame. Only when that has been removed will you be able to see how the webbing is attached. The cross-section (**1**) shows how the layers are constructed. Remove all the tacks holding the webbing in place (**2**). Once you are left with a bare frame, check its condition. If there are a great many tack holes, fill them in with plastic wood. It will help to strengthen the frame if you spread a layer of wood glue over its top surface and allow it to dry before you continue.

Figures 3-8 Attaching the webbing

The whole structure of the seat must be supported by six strips of webbing, three running from side to side and three from back to front, and equally spaced. It is also important that they are all attached to the frame with the same degree of tension.

Measure the frame from front to back and from side to side to determine the central point on each rail (which you should mark with chalk or pencil) and the amount of webbing you will need, allowing for 25 mm (1 in) turnovers at each end of the webbing strips (**3**).

Figure 1

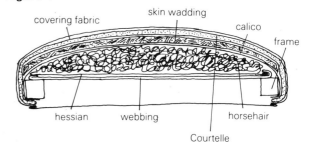

covering fabric
skin wadding
calico
frame
hessian
webbing
horsehair
Courtelle

cross-section

Figure 2

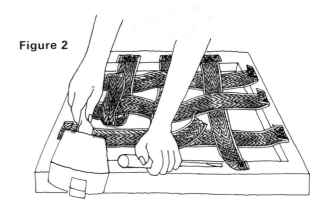

Figure 3

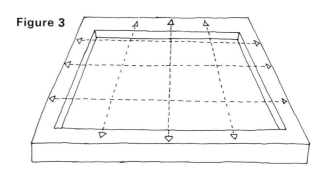

Turn over about 25 mm (1 in) of the end of the roll of webbing and, with the folded side up, attach this end to the centre of the back rail with five 20 mm ($\frac{5}{8}$ in) improved tacks through the two layers. These tacks should be arranged in a W-shape to prevent splitting the wood (**4**). Take a webbing stretcher and push a loop of the webbing through the hole in the stretcher from underneath, with the handle of the stretcher pointing towards the centre of the chair. Place the stretcher bar through the loop (**5**). Stretch the webbing over the front edge of the front rail at the centre, and pull the handle firmly towards you so that the webbing is tight over the frame without having undue stress put on it (**6**).

Figure 4

Figure 5

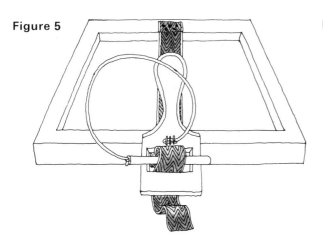

Figure 6

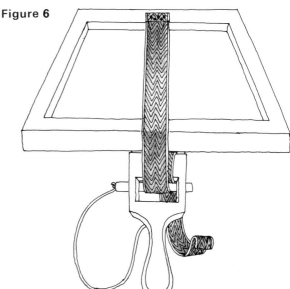

Tilt the frame up slightly from the work surface and hold the top edge of it firmly in one hand, bracing the front edge against the work surface with your knee (**7**). Using a hammer, drive three tacks into the webbing and frame. Cut the webbing so that it extends about 25 mm (1 in) past the edge of the frame, fold it back over the frame and hammer in two more tacks through the double thickness to make what would be a W-shape if all the tacks were visible (see figure 8). Attach two more pieces of webbing to the frame in the same way, on each side of and parallel to the first piece so that they are all equally spaced.

Take the loose end of the roll of webbing, pass it over the first piece of stretched webbing already in place, then under the middle one and over the next. Fold over 25 mm (1 in) and attach to the centre of one of the side rails as shown in figure 4. Stretch and tack it to the centre of the opposite rail. If the side rails are not parallel, fold the webbing so that the folded edge is parallel to the rail rather than at right angles to

Figure 7

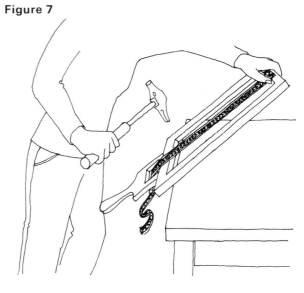

the webbing itself. Attach two more pieces of webbing at either side of and parallel to the first one, weaving them in the opposite way to it (**8**).

Figure 8

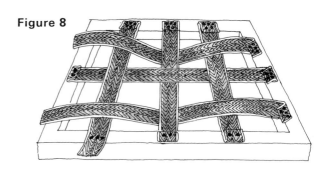

Figures 9-11 Attaching the hessian

Take a piece of 280 or 340 g (10 or 12 oz) hessian 50 mm (2 in) larger all round than the frame. Lay it on the frame which has been placed on a work surface so that the back rail is farthest away from you. Turn up a 25 mm (1 in) hem on the hessian along the length of the back rail and place it so that it just covers the tacks on the webbing. Attach it to the centre of the rail with one 13 mm ($\frac{1}{2}$ in) fine tack. This 'temporary' tack may need to come out again, so do not hammer it flat. To square the hessian, pull it across the frame and again anchor it lightly with a tack directly opposite the first tack (**9**). Put one tack at the centre of each of the other rails in the same way. Pull the hessian taut from corner to corner and secure with another tack at each corner, also driven in lightly. In the same way, place additional tacks between those already in position. Only when you are satisfied that the hessian is positioned straight and taut should you drive all the tacks home. Trim the hessian to approximately 40 mm (1$\frac{1}{2}$ in) outside the tacks (**10**).

Figure 9

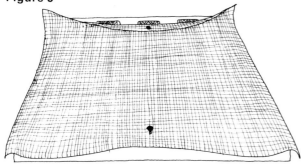

Now turn up a hem all round and tack it down, making sure that the tacks are evenly spaced and about 50 mm (2 in) apart. When you come to the corners, fold one hem over the other and secure with a single tack (**11**).

Figure 10

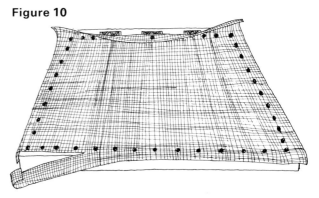

Figure 11

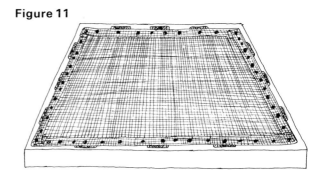

Figures 12-14 Anchoring the horsehair with bridle ties

Thread a springing needle with enough twine to go one and a half times round the perimeter of the seat, and knot the end. Make a small stitch in the hessian 50 mm (2 in) diagonally in from the top left-hand corner. Pull the twine through, make a slip knot and pull it tight. Make another stitch in the top centre, with the needle pointing towards you so that it comes out slightly nearer the centre of the seat (**12**). Leave the loop of twine loose enough to insert, say, a couple of fingers.

At the top right-hand corner make another stitch in the same way (**13**). Make a fourth stitch by the centre of the side rail, and continue stitching round the seat to make loops – the bridle ties – until you reach the point where you started, bringing your stitch out above the first one.

Now make a small stitch in the middle of the seat, at right angles to the direction of the twine, and then make another right-angled stitch at the bottom right-hand corner. Fasten off the twine with a knot and cut (**14**).

Take up a handful of horsehair, tease it out slightly and gently insert it under and around the loops you have just made, as shown in the photograph, so that it makes a firm, even mass about 50 mm (2 in) thick and slightly higher in the middle to form a smooth domed shape. It is very important that there are no lumps or thin patches in evidence, so it is worth spending time making sure that the surface is as even as possible. Any very hard or matted pieces should be removed. Make sure that the horsehair is neatly tucked in around the edges and does not overhang the frame.

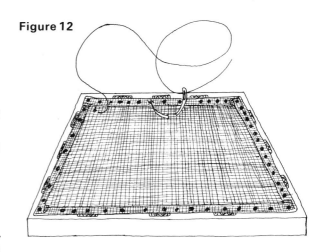
Figure 12

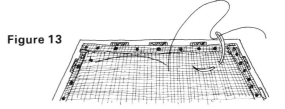
Figure 13

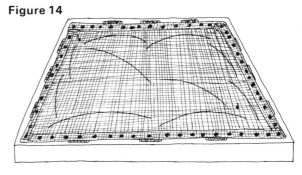
Figure 14

Inserting horsehair around the bridle ties.

Figures 15–21 Attaching the calico

Cut a piece of calico large enough to go over the seat and a good 50 mm (2 in) or so beyond the undersides of the rails.

Turn the seat upside-down and centre it on the calico. Pull the calico up over the front rail and temporarily tack it with a 10 mm ($\frac{3}{8}$ in) fine tack in the centre (**15**). Stretch the calico very tightly

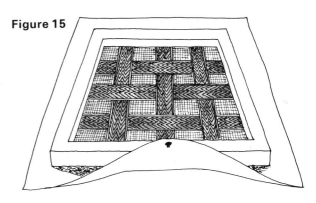
Figure 15

across the seat and secure it with another temporary tack on the opposite side. Attach the calico to the side rails in the same way.

To anchor the corners, begin by lifting each one slightly to free any horsehair (which must not go over the edge of the seat frame since this would prevent it being put back in the chair frame easily.) Pulling the calico tightly over the corner with one hand, ease and smooth it into position with the other (**16**). Keep it in position with one or two temporary tacks. When you have anchored all four corners, turn the seat the right way up and make sure they are rounded and firm and that no wood can be felt from the top of the seat. If necessary, remove the tacks, add more horsehair and retack. Now pull and smooth the calico as tightly as possible along each rail so that no excess hair will be forced down to the sides, and tack it lightly to the frame at 50 mm (2 in) intervals (**17**), leaving the temporary tacks in the corners. Check the padding along the edges as you go, adding more horsehair where necessary.

Figure 16

Figure 17

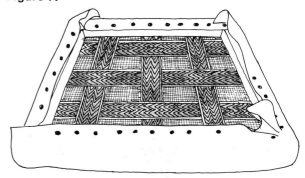

To finish the corners, remove the temporary tack from each one in turn, pull the calico tightly towards the centre of the seat and insert a 10 mm ($\frac{3}{8}$ in) tack firmly about 13 mm ($\frac{1}{2}$ in) in from the corner. Cut into the excess calico at each side of this tack to form a tongue shape (**18**). Pull one side of the calico down over this tongue and anchor it with two tacks about 25 mm (1 in) apart (**19**). Trim the calico to 13 mm ($\frac{1}{2}$ in) from the line of these tacks and to about 50 mm (2 in) along from the corner (**20**). In the same way, anchor the other side at right angles to the first and trim (**21**). Repeat with the other three corners.

Drive home the existing tacks along the rails and add more until they are positioned at about 25 mm (1 in) intervals. Finish trimming the calico to within 13 mm ($\frac{1}{2}$ in) of the tacks. You will now be able to see whether the horsehair is smoothly distributed across the seat. Any minor unevenness can be levelled by rearranging the hair with the point of a regulator needle.

Figure 18

Figure 19

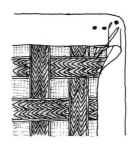

Figure 20

Figure 21

Figures 22 & 23 Preparation for the final covering

Cut a piece of sheet (skin) wadding to exactly the same size as the top of the seat, making sure it does not go over the sides. This wadding prevents the prickly horsehair working through the covering fabric. Lay it over the calico (**22**); then cut a piece of 60 g (2 oz) Courtelle large enough to go over the seat to the underside of the frame. Turn the frame upside-down and place over the Courtelle centrally. With 10 mm ($\frac{3}{8}$ in) fine tacks, tightly anchor the Courtelle in place all round, stretching and pulling it at each corner to avoid bulk (**23**). Mark the front and back centres on the edge of the Courtelle with chalk or pencil.

Figure 24 The final covering

Cut a piece of covering fabric large enough to go over the seat to the underside of the frame, adding an extra 50 mm (2 in) all round. Make sure that any pattern is centred. Mark the middle of both front and back with a tiny nick. Place this in a centred position on the top of your seat and turn the whole thing over (**24**). Pull the covering fabric over the rails at the front and back, aligning the nicks with the chalk marks on the Courtelle. Insert a 10 mm ($\frac{3}{8}$ in) fine tack temporarily at both these points. Place a similar tack at the centre of each side rail. Attach the fabric to the rails in exactly the same way as you did with the calico (figures 16–21). At the corners, you may find it easier to trim away more fabric than you did with the calico to make two neat pleats at each corner.

Figure 25 Finishing off

Cut a piece of closely woven black upholstery linen (or hessian) 40 mm ($1\frac{1}{2}$ in) larger all round than the flat underside of the seat. Turn under a 6 mm ($\frac{1}{4}$ in) hem and, using 13 mm ($\frac{1}{2}$ in) fine tacks, fasten the linen down over the existing tacks, first putting one in lightly at the centre of each rail, then one in near each end. If you think the fabric is straight and taut, drive these tacks home. Put in more tacks, firmly this time, along the rails at approximately 25 mm (1 in) intervals, making simple square corners with turned edges (**25**).

Figure 22

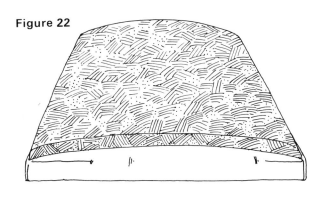

Figure 23

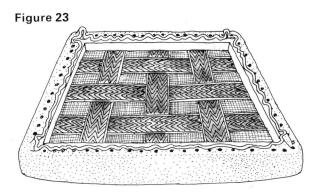

Figure 24

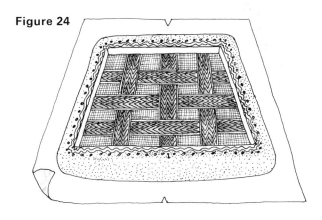

Figure 25

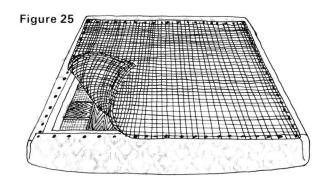

Project 3
Non-sprung stool

Introduction

The method used to upholster this stool is similar to that which might be used for a simple non-sprung chair. The most important new technique introduced here is that of making a reinforced roll of padding round the stool's edge.

The structure of the edge roll is used on most upholstered furniture; it protects the edge against wear, covers and softens the wooden frame, and provides a surround for the soft padding in the middle of the seat, where most of the sitter's weight will fall.

Apart from this important new feature, the basic structure of webbing, hessian, padding and several layers of covering is the same as that described for project 2.

Tools

mallet
ripping chisel
scissors or sharp knife
webbing stretcher
hammer
file
felt-tipped pen
springing needle
double bayonet needle
regulator needle (or large bradawl)
four upholstery or kitchen skewers

Materials

black and white (first-quality) webbing: see project 2, figure 3 for measurements and add 500 mm (20 in)

20 mm ($\frac{5}{8}$ in) improved tacks

280 or 340 g (10 or 12 oz) hessian — a piece slightly larger than the top of the stool

scrim — four pieces, one for each side of the frame, each 150 mm (6 in) wide and 100 mm (4 in) longer than the side to which it will be attached, for the edge roll

twine (upholsterer's twine is always sold by the reel)

ginger fibre — use the old stuffing to estimate quantities

10 mm ($\frac{3}{8}$ in) fine tacks

horsehair: gauge approximately how much you need from the old stuffing

sheet (skin) wadding: enough to cover the top of the stool

60 g (2 oz) Courtelle: see figure 32 for the amount needed

covering fabric — enough to go over the top of the stool to the underside of the frame

black upholstery linen or hessian: a piece slightly larger than the underside of your stool

Removing the old upholstery

Using a mallet and a ripping chisel, and working always in the direction of the wood's grain, remove all the tacks holding the old upholstery in place. Detailed instructions for doing this are given in project 2, figure 1. As all upholsterers work in slightly different ways the layers may not be exactly as described, but it is always a good idea to examine carefully each layer of material and padding as you remove it, to see how the work was done originally and to help you estimate quantities. Keep the old top cover and use it as a pattern from which to cut your new covering fabric. If the horsehair is still in good condition you may be able to reuse it.

Figures 1 & 2 Attaching the webbing and hessian

Figure 1

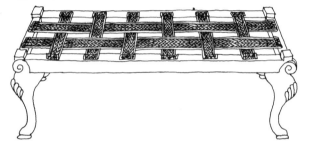

Keeping the frame level and preferably on a raised surface so that all parts of it are easily accessible, tack strips of webbing firmly to the four rails of the frame, using a webbing stretcher and suitable hammer, and spacing the strips approximately their own width apart (**1**). Instructions for this procedure are given in detail in project 2. figures 3–8. Place the hessian over the webbing, position it straight and taut, and attach it to the frame (**2**), as described in project 2, figures 9–11.

Figure 2

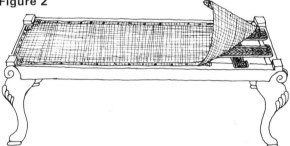

Figure 3 Preparing the rails

With a large file, smooth away any sharp right angles at the top outside edges of the rails (**3**), to make a sloping surface at least 6 mm ($\frac{1}{4}$ in) wide all round the edge of the frame, into which tacks can be driven. This procedure is called chamfering or bevelling.

Figure 3

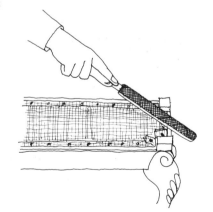

Figures 4-28 Constructing a reinforced edge roll

Since a stool will receive the same amount of wear on all sides, it must be padded so that it looks and wears the same on all four edges, and the most effective way of doing this is to make the edge roll quite separately from the main padding, to go all the way round the stool. The roll is made with a strong material called scrim which is stuffed with fibre to form a sausage shape. This is then reinforced with one row each of two types of stitching: blind stitching and top stitching.

Figures 4-10 Attaching the scrim to the hessian

With a felt-tipped pen, mark out a border on the hessian 75 mm (3 in) in from the edges along all four sides, as a guide for the edge roll (**4**).

Cut four pieces of scrim (one for each side of the frame) 150 mm (6 in) wide and each one about 100 mm (4 in) longer than the side to which it will be attached. Turn under a 13 mm ($\frac{1}{2}$ in) hem on the first piece of scrim, and place this fold along the border line you have drawn on the hessian, so that the raw edge of the scrim faces away from the centre of the stool. Anchor each end with a temporary tack.

Thread a 75 mm (3 in) springing needle with more than enough twine to go round the stool. Make a stitch in the scrim and hessian at one end of a rail, at the point where the two border lines meet (**5**). Pull the twine through almost to the end and fasten it with a slip knot. Make another stitch 13 mm ($\frac{1}{2}$ in) from the first one, and continue making neat 13 mm ($\frac{1}{2}$ in) running stitches along the length of the border line (**6**), being careful not to catch the webbing in the stitches.

Stop stitching when you reach the next border line (**7**), but do not finish off or cut the twine. Trim this end of the scrim to 25 mm (1 in) beyond the edge of the stool and remove the temporary tack. Lift up this loose end of the scrim and place the second piece along the second side exactly as you did with the first, having turned under a hem. Anchor this second strip with temporary tacks (**8**) and continue your running stitch at right angles to the first line of stitches without breaking the twine (**9**).

Continue in this way until all four pieces of scrim have been sewn round the four sides of the frame (**10**). Pull the twine through to the underside, knot it and cut it off. Remove all temporary tacks.

Figure 4

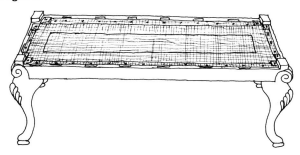

Figure 5   **Figure 6**

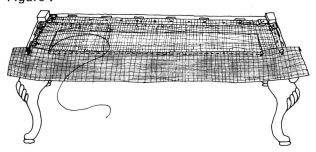

Figure 7

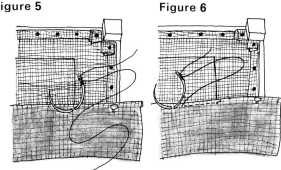

Figure 8   **Figure 9**

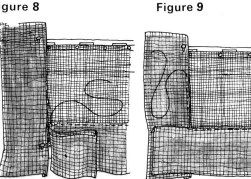

Figure 10

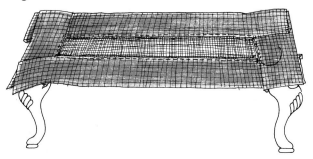

Figures 11–17 Padding the scrim with fibre

The next stage is to make bridle ties which will keep the fibre in position in the edge roll. Thread the springing needle with a piece of twine long enough to go round the stool about one and a half times. Make a slip knot in one corner of the hessian at a point 40 mm (1½ in) outside the border marking, under the scrim you have just attached. Make loops about 150 mm (6 in) long, beginning each one just before the end of the previous one (similar to those in project 2, figures 12–14) and running them round the stool between the border line and the edge of the hessian (**11**). When you reach the starting point, finish off with a knot and cut the twine.

Tease out a handful of ginger fibre and, starting at one end of a rail, slip it under and around the first loop. Add another handful under this same loop (**12**), pull the scrim over the fibre to the edge of the rail and make sure it feels firm, looks nicely rounded and does not flatten under pressure. Continue in this way until all the scrim has been firmly padded.

Using 10 mm (⅜ in) fine tacks and starting in the centre of one long rail, pull the scrim over the fibre, turn under a 13 mm (½ in) hem and put a temporary tack through the scrim into the chamfered edge. Work outwards towards the ends of the rail, putting in temporary tacks at 50 mm (2 in) intervals (**13**). Do the same along the other three rails, leaving the corners open for the moment. If you are satisfied that the edge roll is even, rounded and firm, drive the tacks home. If there are any bare patches under the scrim take out the tacks at that place, add more fibre and then drive the tacks home. To make the surface even, insert the sharp end of a regulator needle (or a large bradawl) through the scrim and gently move it around in the fibre in order to smooth it out and distribute it evenly.

At each corner, pull back the two layers of scrim (**14**) and add a little extra fibre under that which is already there, for increased firmness. Now stretch the bottom layer of scrim over the top and sides of the fibre, fold the edge under and anchor it along the frame with permanent tacks (**15**); then fold the top layer of scrim diagonally under from the inner to the outer corner (**16**). Pull tight and tack down at the corner, and then turn down the remaining edge to neaten and tack it down (**17**). Use the regulator needle to smooth the filling.

Figure 11

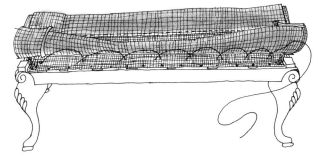

Figure 12

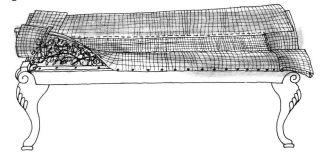

Figure 13

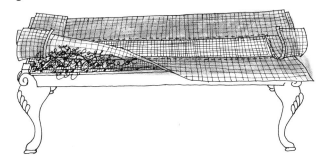

Figure 14

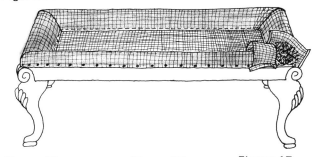

Figure 15   Figure 16   Figure 17

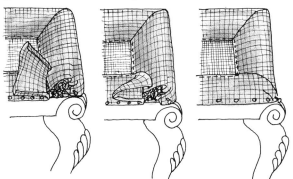

Figures 18-24 Blind stitching

The purpose of blind stitches — sometimes called 'sink' stitches — is to bring the stuffing firmly towards the outside edges of the stool by catching it in loops of twine, as shown in the cross-section (**18**). Thread a 250 mm (10 in) double bayonet needle with enough twine to go one and a half times round the perimeter of the stool. Working from right to left, insert the needle into the outside of one corner, about 6 mm ($\frac{1}{4}$ in) above the rail and pointing it diagonally towards the centre of the stool (**19**). Pass it through the stuffing and scrim so that about 150 mm (6 in) protrudes at the other side, but do not pull it right through: the eye of the needle should now be inside the roll, about three-quarters of the way through the stuffing. Now manipulate the eye of the needle towards the right (inside the roll to catch the stuffing) and then push it back towards you so that it comes out 6 mm ($\frac{1}{4}$ in) to the right of the starting point (**20**). Fasten the end of the twine with a slip knot, but do not cut.

Insert the needle about 50 mm (2 in) to the left of the original point of entry, pushing it straight into the roll (**21**) until the eye of the needle is about three-quarters of the way through the stuffing. Bring the eye out again halfway between the two stitches (**22**), pull the twine taut, and make a knot by looping each end of the twine twice round the needle (**23** and **24**) so that the stitches do not loosen. Withdraw the needle completely and continue stitching round the stool, pushing the needle in at 50 mm (2 in) intervals, and returning it 25 mm (1 in) further back from the previous stitch. Use a regulator every two or three stitches to work the stuffing forwards as evenly as possible. When you get to the corners the needle should be pushed in so that it points diagonally towards the centre of the stool. When you have made the last stitch, knot the twine and cut it.

Figure 18

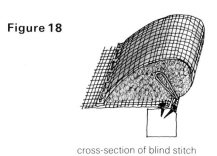

cross-section of blind stitch

Figure 19

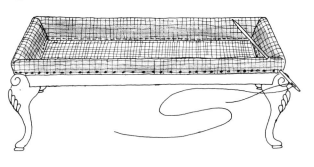

Figure 20

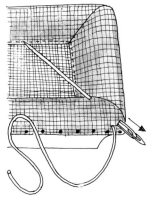

Figure 21

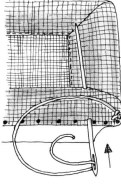

Figure 22

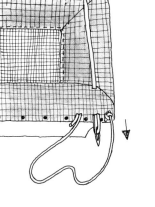

Figure 23

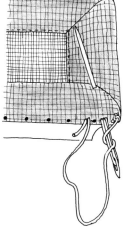

Figure 24

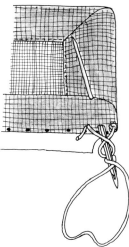

Figures 25-28 Top stitching

These stitches are similar to blind stitches, except that the needle is pulled all the way through the stuffing so that it forms a line of stitches on both sides of the edge roll. When pulled tight, these stitches should form a firm roll about the thickness of a thumb along the top, as shown in the cross-section (**25**).

Thread the double bayonet needle with enough twine to go one and a half times round the stool. Working from right to left again, above the row of blind stitches, start by securing the end of the twine with a slip knot as in figure 20.

Now insert the needle exactly as if you were going to make a blind stitch (see figure 21), but this time pull the needle right through the edge roll to the other side. Now push the eye of the needle back through the roll at a point about 25 mm (1 in) to the right of where it went in until the needle is in the position shown (**26**). Loop the twine as before (**27**) and withdraw the needle to the outside edge, pulling the twine forward and in the direction that your stitches are running, to tighten the knot. Continue stitching in this way, making sure that the line of stitches and knots runs parallel to the edge of the roll (**28**).

You will need to use the regulator frequently to get a firm roll of even height and thickness. (Making both top and blind stitches is a fairly tricky and time-consuming job, but they are two of the most important techniques of upholstery.)

Figures 29-36 Padding and covering

Figures 29 & 30 Making bridle ties and anchoring the horsehair

Using a springing needle and twine, make a small stitch at one corner of the hessian now enclosed by the edge roll. Secure it with a slip knot and make bridle ties (see project 2, figures 12–14) in a zig-zag pattern (**29**). Tease out the horsehair in the same way as you did with the ginger fibre and tuck it under and around the bridle ties to fill the central part of the stool with a firm, even layer of horsehair. Make this more thickly padded in the middle (**30**), so that it is slightly domed in shape.

Figure 25

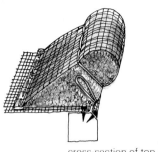

cross-section of top stitch

Figure 26   **Figure 27**

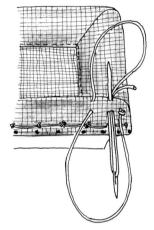 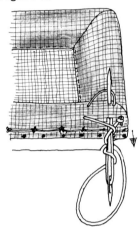

Figure 28

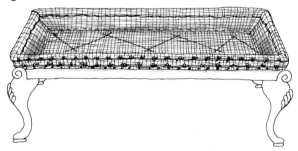

Figure 29

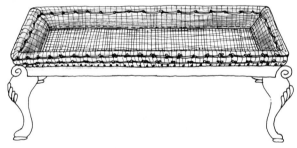

Figure 30

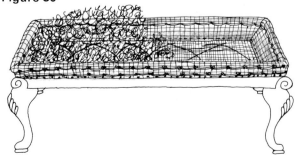

Figures 31 & 32 Preparation for the final covering

Cut a piece of sheet (skin) wadding large enough to go over the top of the stool and slightly over the edge roll. Lay it over the horsehair (**31**) and anchor each corner with a skewer stuck in straight, at right angles to the top.

Cut a piece of 60 g (2 oz) Courtelle large enough to cover the stool and fasten underneath the side rails, and lay it over the top of the stool. With 10 mm ($\frac{3}{8}$ in) fine tacks, tack it down near the bottom of the side edge of each rail, removing the skewers as you come to each corner. When you are doing this, remember to stretch and smooth the Courtelle carefully, making sure no horsehair escapes from under the wadding. Trim at the bottom edge of the rails (**32**).

Figures 33–36 The final covering and finishing off

Centring the pattern if necessary, cut a piece of covering fabric the same size as the Courtelle and lay it on the stool. Fasten it down with a temporary tack at the centre of each rail and another near both ends of each rail (**33**), making sure that the fabric is straight and smooth. Put in more temporary tacks all round at 25 mm (1 in) intervals, pulling the fabric taut and stopping about 75 mm (3 in) short of the corners. Once you have made any minor adjustments necessary and you are satisfied that the cover is smooth and straight, drive the tacks home.

At the corners, ease the fabric so it fits as neatly as possible round the legs, making a small pleat if necessary. Anchor the fabric with a closely spaced row of tacks (**34**). Trim the fabric as close to the tacks as possible all round (**35**).

Cover the tacks by gluing a strip of braid or gimp over them at the corners and along the bottom edge of the four side rails (**36**).

Turn the stool over and cover the bottom with a piece of black upholstery linen or hessian using the technique described in project 2, figure 25.

Figure 31

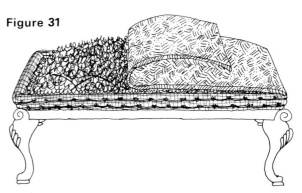

Figure 32

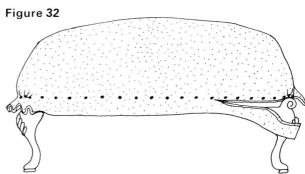

Figure 33

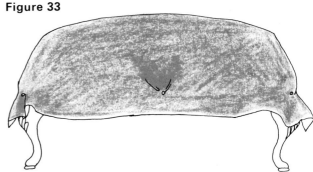

Figure 34

Figure 35

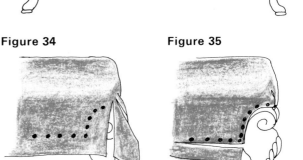

Figure 36

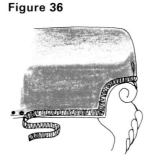

Project 4
Sprung dining chair

Introduction

This project introduces the basic and important technique of springing. The way in which the springs are anchored (or lashed) to the frame and to each other will determine the degree of comfort and support provided by the chair as well as its appearance and durability.

The procedure involved is not difficult but it does require concentration, and you will need to practise before you are able to do it quickly and well. You should get used to working with springs on a fairly small project such as this before you attempt anything larger and more complex, even though the basic skills remain the same. It is worth taking time to work very slowly — even to redo certain steps if necessary — until you are totally satisfied with the result and feel familiar with the techniques. The chair shown here has five springs, but some have only three and others as many as nine; make sure that, however many springs you are working with, they are evenly spaced over the seat area.

The reinforced edge roll is another important feature of this project. Although the most complicated part of it, the stitching, remains the same as for the stool, the padding in this instance is applied in one stage evenly over the entire seat, then pulled to the edges; the edge roll is not made separately from the central area of padding. When you are working on a chair (as opposed to a stool), the two methods are interchangeable — use whichever you find easier.

As always, it is important to remove the old upholstery carefully. Working with a mallet and chisel and following the procedure outlined in project 2, remove all the layers until you are left with the bare frame. You will find it useful to keep the old padding so that you can refer to its structure as you work.

Tools

mallet
ripping chisel
scissors
webbing stretcher
hammer
springing needle
double bayonet needle
regulator needle
tailor's chalk

Materials

black and white (first-quality) webbing: see figure 1 for measurements and add 500 mm (20 in)

20 mm ($\frac{5}{8}$ in) improved tacks

five 100 mm (4 in) gauge 10 double-cone springs: you will probably be able to use the ones you have removed from the chair

twine (upholsterer's twine is always sold by the reel)

laid cord (also sold by the reel)

280 or 340 g (10 or 12 oz) hessian — one piece slightly larger than the seat frame

13 mm ($\frac{1}{2}$ in) fine tacks

horsehair — use the old stuffing to gauge approximately how much you need

scrim — one piece large enough to go over the padded seat and fasten to the outside faces of the seat frame

sheet (skin) wadding — one piece the same size as the top of the seat

covering fabric — enough to cover the padded seat and attach to the outside faces of the seat frame

braid or gimp — enough to go round the seat frame

Project 4

Figure 1 Attaching the webbing

Following the instructions given for attaching webbing in project 2, figures 3–8, tack six pieces of webbing underneath the frame, making sure the central pieces in both rows are straight and at right angles to each other. If the frame is wider at the front than the back, the strips of webbing running from side to side should be parallel to the front and back rails and to each other, while the side strips of webbing running from front to back should be parallel to the side rails (**1**).

Figure 1

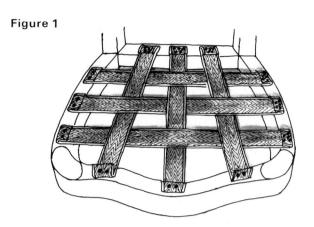

Figures 2–5 Attaching the springs to the webbing

Stand the chair upright, and place five 100 mm (4 in) gauge 10 galvanized steel double-cone springs in position at the junctions of the webbing, so that the knots at the top of the springs are facing the centre of the chair (**2**).

Figure 2

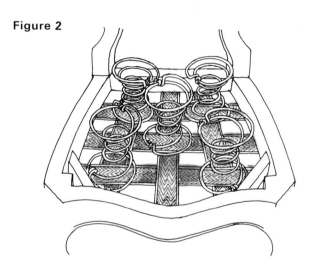

You should attach each spring to the webbing with three equidistant stitches around the base of the spring. To do this, thread a springing needle with approximately 2 m (78 in) of twine. With the chair facing you, insert your needle into the webbing from underneath, at the base of the spring at the top left-hand corner. Catch the spring in a single stitch and push the needle back through to the underside of the webbing. Fasten the twine with a slip knot. Bring your needle up again, make a second stitch over the base of the spring and, when your needle is back on the underside of the webbing, knot the twine to the long stitch just formed. Make the third stitch (**3** and **4**) in the same way. Repeat this procedure for all the springs, working in the shape of a Z from the first spring to the last (**5**). Finish off with a double knot.

Figure 3   Figure 4

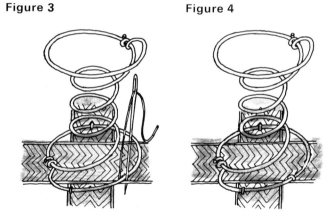

Figure 5

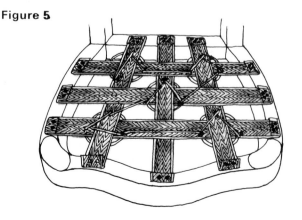

Figures 6–12 Lashing the springs

The purpose of this process (also called cording) is to keep the springs upright and under tension, so that when the chair is sat on they are all depressed together.

Drive in three 15 mm ($\frac{5}{8}$ in) temporary tacks along each rail in line with the centre of each spring (see figure 11). Cut six pieces of laid cord long enough to go very generously across the frame, over the tops of the springs. Make a single knot at the end of one piece and slip it over one of the temporary tacks (**6**). Make another single knot (**7**), pull it tight and drive the tack home (**8**). Attach all six pieces of cord along two adjoining rails in this way (see figure 8).

The springs must be lashed so that the top coil of the outer ones leans towards its nearest corner, making an overall domed shape (the central spring remains upright). Starting with one of the pieces of cord on the side rail, make a simple knot (**9**) round the nearest point of the top coil of the nearest spring, pulling the cord tightly so the spring leans a little towards the rail. Then make a half-hitch knot on the top coil opposite the first knot (**10**). Take the cord to the next spring in a straight line, and knot it with a half hitch. Compress the springs about 13 mm ($\frac{1}{2}$ in); this will loosen the two half hitches and you should now tighten the cord, taking up the slack so that the springs stay under a slight degree of tension. Then make another simple knot opposite the second half hitch. Anchor the cord to the appropriate temporary tack with two single knots, pulling it so that the top coil of the second spring leans toward the nearest rail at the same angle as the first spring (**11**). Trim the cord.

Lash the second row of two springs in the same way and parallel to the first, then lash the central spring using two simple knots. Compress it as much as the other four springs, but keep it upright. Now lash the central spring from front to back, looping the cord round the existing lashing where the two cords cross, before making your second knot.

Lash the outer springs from front to back, knotting as before and looping the cord round the existing lashing as you cross it.

When you have finished this lashing, all five springs should be compressed equally, the top coil of each outer spring leaning toward its corner and the central one remaining upright (**12**).

Figure 6 **Figure 7** **Figure 8**

Figure 9 **Figure 10**

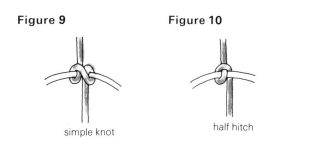

simple knot   half hitch

Figure 11

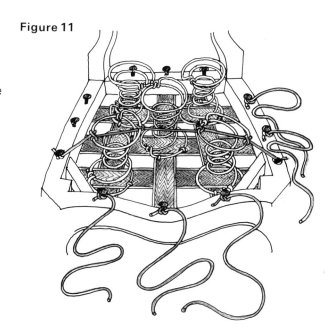

Figure 12

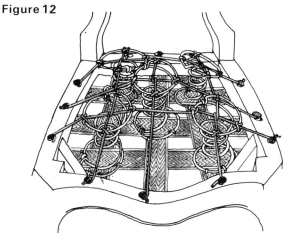

Figures 13-17 Attaching the hessian to the frame

Cut a piece of 340 g (12 oz) hessian 100 mm (4 in) larger all round than the seat of the chair. Turn up a 13 mm ($\frac{1}{2}$ in) hem along one edge and anchor it to the back of the frame with a 13 mm ($\frac{1}{2}$ in) fine temporary tack at the centre of the rail. Pull the hessian taut over the springs and fasten it with a temporary tack at the centre of the front rail. Repeat from side rail to side rail (**13**).

At this stage, you will be able to see from the level and angles of the springs whether they have been properly lashed, and you should make any necessary adjustments to the lashing before you continue. When you are quite satisfied with the springs, drive the tacks home.

Make a diagonal cut into the hessian at the two back corners so that it can be folded round the two upright rails of the chair back. Tack round these corners (**14**), then tack along all four seat rails at 50 mm (2 in) intervals. Trim the three sides of the hessian which do not yet have a hem to 13 mm ($\frac{1}{2}$ in) beyond the frame (**15**), then turn up a hem and tack it to the frame, putting the tacks between those which are already in place (**16** and **17**).

Figure 13

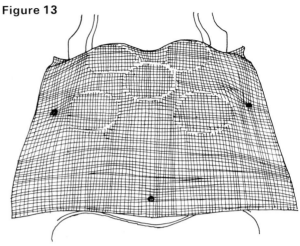

Figure 14

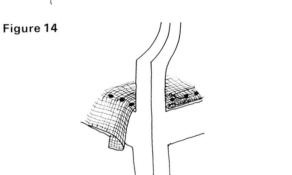

Figure 15

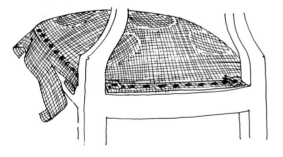

Figure 16

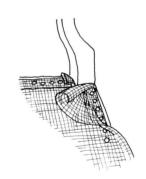

Figure 17

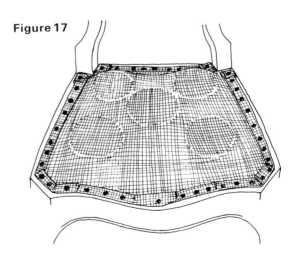

Figure 18 Attaching the hessian to the springs

The springs must now be attached to the hessian in exactly the same pattern as they were to the webbing, that is, with stitches at three equidistant positions round the top coil.

Thread a piece of twine approximately 1·5 m (60 in) long through a springing needle. Starting at the back left-hand corner, insert the needle into the hessian and bring it out again, catching the front of the spring underneath. Tie this tightly with a slip knot. Take the twine to the back of the spring and catch and secure it in a half hitch. Bring the needle back to the front of the spring and catch the spring once more so that the twine forms an inverted V-shape on the hessian. Repeat this procedure with the right-hand back spring, then the central one and then the two front ones (**18**). Fasten the last stitch with a double knot and cut the twine.

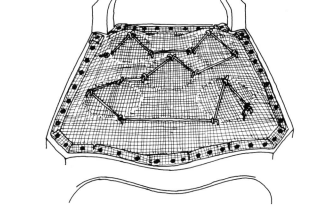

Figure 18

Figure 19 The first set of bridle ties and first layer of horsehair

Thread the springing needle with a piece of twine long enough to go about one and a half times round the perimeter of the seat. Make bridle ties round and across the seat as described in project 2, figures 12–14.

Take a handful of horsehair and tuck it under the first loop of twine, working it under and around the loop and pressing it down firmly (**19**). Continue adding more hair and pressing it down until it feels firm and thick. Fill all the ties, blending the hair together so that the surface is smooth and even. Add more hair to the centre of the seat, blending it with the surrounding hair. Continue adding to it until the seat feels solid and you cannot detect the springs.

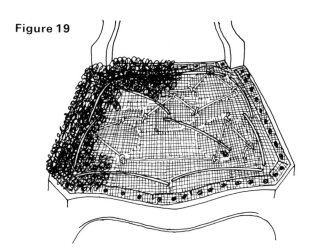

Figure 19

Figure 20 Attaching the scrim to the frame

Measure the distance from one bottom edge of the frame, over the horsehair, to the bottom of the opposite edge at the widest point. Add 50 mm (2 in) all round and cut a piece of scrim this size. Lay it over the hair and tack it neatly with 15 mm ($\frac{5}{8}$ in) improved tacks temporarily to the centre of the outer faces of the four rails (**20**). Adjust if necessary, drive the tacks home and, working from the centre outwards, secure with more tacks spaced about 40 mm (1$\frac{1}{2}$ in) apart (see figure 21). Cut into the scrim at the back corners and fold it under to neaten.

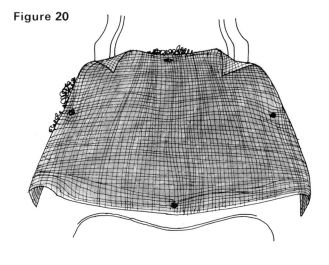

Figure 20

Figure 21 Anchoring the padding

Thread a double bayonet needle with a piece of twine 1·5 m (60 in) long. Make a stitch in the scrim 75 mm (3 in) in from the left side of the frame at the back and secure with a slip knot. Push the needle down through the seat, avoiding the springs, to the bottom of the chair, so that the eye of the needle just clears the hessian. Then push it straight up so the other point of the needle comes out about 13 mm ($\frac{1}{2}$ in) away from the point of entry on the top of the seat. Knot, but do not cut, the twine. Repeat this stitch at the centre of each rail and at each corner, keeping 75 mm (3 in) in from the rails as shown. Knot and cut the twine (**21**). Turn up the excess scrim all round the edges of the seat, tack it down between the first row of tacks, and trim (see figure 22).

Figures 22 & 23 Reinforcing the edges

To ensure that there is sufficient padding round the edges where it is most needed, and to cover the hard rail, the edges of the chair should be reinforced with blind stitches (**22**) and top stitches (**23**) in a manner very similar to that used for the stool in project 3, figures 18–28. Manipulate the hair towards the outer edges with a regulator needle, keeping the surface smooth and even.

Figure 24 The second layer of padding

The edge roll you have just formed makes the chair seat somewhat saucer-shaped; the depression must be filled in so that the edge is not detectable as a separate entity.

On the scrim, make another set of bridle ties slightly tighter than the first set — make them loose enough to be able to put just your thumb under them. Insert a layer of horsehair about 25 mm (1 in) thick under and around these ties (**24**), making sure you do not go over the reinforced edge and that the surface is smooth, even and slightly domed.

Figure 25 Attaching the skin wadding and the calico

Cut a piece of sheet (skin) wadding slightly larger all round than the top of the seat and lay it in position.

Now cut a piece of calico approximately 100 mm (4 in) larger all around than the top of the seat. Anchor this with three temporary tacks to the

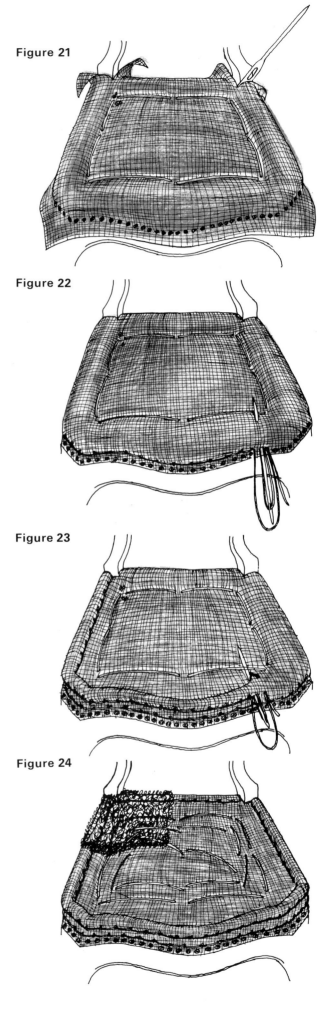

Figure 21

Figure 22

Figure 23

Figure 24

outer face of one rail at the centre, pull it taut across the chair and fasten it with three more temporary tacks to the centre of the opposite rail. Repeat across the other two rails. Neaten at both back corners by making a diagonal cut towards the centre of the seat (**25**), turning the calico under and tacking it neatly round the chair back. If necessary, use your regulator needle to neaten and tuck it in. This chair has very gently rounded corners at the front, over which the calico can be stretched and tacked in a straightforward way. See below for how to pleat round square or more sharply rounded corners. Drive home the temporary tacks in the centre of the rails and add more, spaced about 25 mm (1 in) apart.

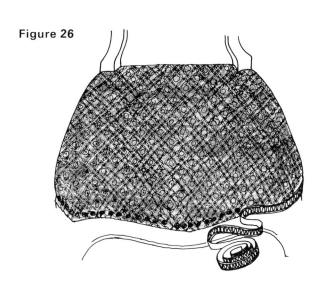

Figure 25

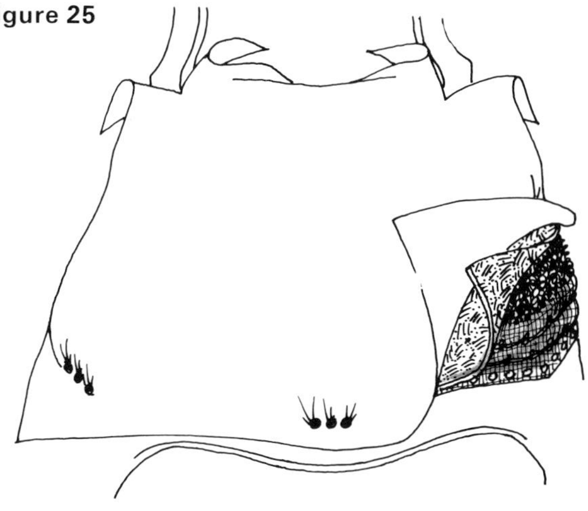

Figure 26 Finishing off

Cut a piece of covering fabric 25 mm (1 in) larger all round than the measurement from the bottom face of one rail, over the seat and across to the bottom face of the opposite rail at the widest part, making sure that any pattern is centred. Measure and mark the centre of the front and back rails. Make a small nick at the centre front and back of the fabric and place it over the seat, aligning the nicks with the central points marked on the rails. Anchor the fabric with three temporary tacks at the centre back. Pull taut and proceed exactly as you did with the calico cover (see figure 25).

Conceal the tacks and raw edges with a length of suitable braid or gimp (trimming) glued on and turned under at the ends (**26**).

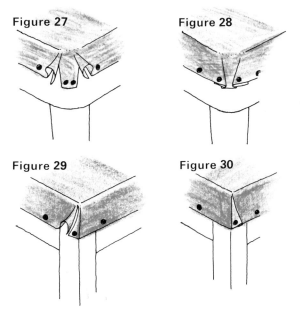

Figure 26

Figures 27 & 28 Finishing rounded corners with a double pleat

Pull the fabric down over each corner and tack it there securely, making sure there is an equal amount of fabric on each side of the tacking point. Fold this fabric to form two pleats facing towards the corner. Cut away any excess material (**27**), pull both pleats taut and secure each one with a tack (**28**).

Figure 27

Figure 28

Figures 29 & 30 Finishing square corners with a single pleat

Pull all the loose fabric at each corner round to one side and fix it there with a tack. Cut away any excess fabric (**29**), leaving enough to pull back to the other side of the corner, making a pleat over the first tack. Put in a second tack (**30**), then slip-stitch down the fold, concealing the stitches on the inside.

Figure 29

Figure 30

Project 5
Occasional chair

Introduction

This Edwardian occasional chair has a fully sprung seat which should be upholstered according to the instructions given for the sprung dining chair (project 4). There may be more springs in a chair of this type since the seat area is usually quite large, but this does not affect the techniques involved.

The new feature of this project is the simple, non-sprung padding on small areas of the arms and back, which provides some degree of comfort while leaving the carved and inlaid wood (called 'show' wood) as the main visual feature of the piece. In order to display this to its best advantage, you should choose a fabric in a plain colour or one with a small subdued pattern.

When you buy the braid or gimp for covering the tack heads, ask your retailer's advice, since there are some types specially designed to go smoothly and neatly round fairly sharp curves like these.

To remove the old padding, use a mallet and a ripping chisel in the usual way, taking great care not to damage the areas of exposed wood. If your chair is very old and has delicate carving like this one, you may find it more satisfactory to use the tip of a small screwdriver, bradawl or regulator needle to work the tacks loose. Be very gentle as you do this, since one hard knock against the frame might split the wood.

Tools

mallet
ripping chisel
scissors
webbing stretcher
hammer
springing needle
double bayonet needle
regulator needle

Materials

black and white (first-quality) webbing: see instructions for measurements and add 500 mm (20 in)

20 mm ($\frac{5}{8}$ in) improved tacks

100 mm (4 in) gauge 10 double-cone springs (the number will vary according to the size of your chair — you will probably be able to use the ones you have removed)

twine (upholsterer's twine is always sold by the reel)

laid cord (also sold by the reel)

280 or 340 g (10 or 12 oz) hessian — three pieces, one slightly larger than the seat frame, and two slightly larger than the back padding

13 mm ($\frac{1}{2}$ in) fine tacks

horsehair — use the old stuffing to gauge how much you need

sheet (skin) wadding — enough to cover the top of the seat, the arm pads and back pad

scrim — three pieces, one large enough to go over the padded seat and fasten to the outside faces of the seat frame, and two large enough to cover the areas of arm padding

covering fabric — enough to cover the padded seat and attach to the outside faces of the seat frame, to go over each arm pad and to cover the back pad (on the inside and the outside of the back)

braid or gimp — enough to go round the seat frame, the arm pads and the back pad, inside and out

ginger fibre for padding the arms — use the old stuffing to estimate quantities

Courtelle — four pieces, two large enough to cover the arm pads and two the same size as the back pad

linter felt — enough to cover the back pad

Project 5

Figures 1–8 Padding the arms

Cut a piece of scrim three times the width of the arm pad area and twice its length. Cut a piece of twine about 75 mm (3 in) longer than the arm pad area. Put in a temporary tack at one end of this area, knot the twine round it and drive it home. Repeat the process with another tack at the other end, making the twine loose enough to be able to pull it about 40 mm ($1\frac{1}{2}$ in) away from the arm at its centre (**1**).

Turn under a 13 mm ($\frac{1}{2}$ in) hem along one side of the scrim and tack it along one side of the area to be padded. Fold the scrim back and tuck handfuls of ginger fibre under and around the twine until you have a tightly packed layer of fibre about 65 mm ($2\frac{1}{2}$ in) thick along the length of the twine. Pull the scrim over this layer and temporarily tack it down in the middle of the other side, turning under another hem (**2**). If the fibre does not feel smooth and firm under the scrim, add some more and then put more temporary tacks along the arm to anchor the scrim (**3**), adding more fibre where necessary. If the fibre still feels lumpy, insert the point of a regulator needle into it and work it around until the surface is smooth.

Pull the scrim over the fibre at one end, turn under a hem and put in temporary tacks at each side of this end, trimming and folding the scrim neatly at the corners. Repeat at the other end.

Check your padding for symmetry, firmness and smoothness. If any adjustment is needed, remove some or all of the tacks and add, remove or rearrange the fibre as necessary. When you are satisfied with the look and feel of the padding, drive the tacks home. In order to make sure the pad keeps its shape, sew a row of top stitches round it as described in project 3, figures 24–26.

Press a thin layer of horsehair over the top of the hessian to fill in the bumps and hollows formed by the top stitches (**4**). Now cut a piece of sheet (skin) wadding the same size and shape as the top of your padding and lay it over the horsehair.

Cut a piece of Courtelle large enough to cover the padding and be attached to the arm rail below it (**5**). Anchor it with a temporary tack halfway along one side, then along the other side, then at each side of both ends and finally all along the sides. Adjust if necessary and drive the tacks home in the usual way.

Figure 1

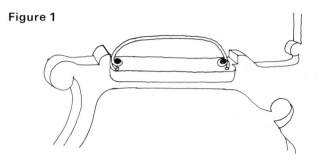

Figure 2

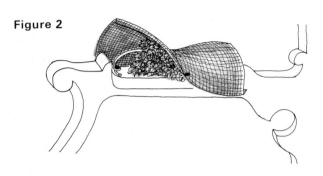

Figure 3

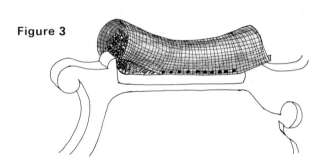

Figure 4

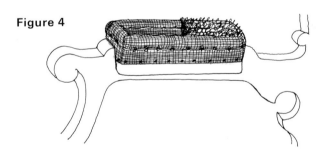

Figure 5

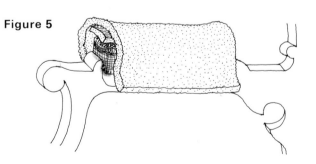

Cut a piece of covering fabric slightly larger than the Courtelle. Anchor it with temporary tacks to one side of the arm rail, pull it over the padding and put in more temporary tacks along the other side, as for the Courtelle.

At each end of the fabric, make a V-shaped cut from the middle to the outside edges of the arm rail where the padding begins, as shown (**6**). Fold the fabric neatly at the corners, trim it if necessary and tuck it down between the wood and the padding with the point of the regulator needle (**7**). Finish the corners according to the instructions for square corners in project 4 (figures 29 & 30). Check for neatness and drive all the temporary tacks home. Glue on a length of braid or gimp to hide them (**8**).

Figures 9–11 Padding the back

Begin by laying the chair on its back so that you can work on a flat surface. Cut a piece of 340 g (12 oz) hessian slightly larger than the area to be padded. Tack it down along one side, beginning with one tack in the middle and spacing the tacks 50–75 mm (2–3 in) apart. Pull taut to the opposite side and anchor, then fill in this side with tacks. Repeat at top and bottom, and trim the hessian as closely as possible to the tacks.

Cut or tear a piece of linter felt the same size as the opening and lay it on top of the hessian; no anchoring is necessary (**9**). Cut a piece of skin wadding slightly larger than the area being padded and tack it down in the same way as you did the hessian. Trim close to the tacks (see figure 10). Cut, tack and trim a layer of Courtelle in the same way (**10**).

To attach the covering fabric, cut it slightly larger than the padded area, turn under a small hem and tack it down in the same way as all the layers of padding, but instead of tacking it permanently immediately, anchor it with temporary tacks so that you can adjust it if necessary. When you are satisfied with it, drive all the tacks home, then cover them with a glued-on length of braid or gimp (**11**).

Treat the outside back in the same way as the front, except that you do not need to add a layer of linter felt for softness.

Figure 6

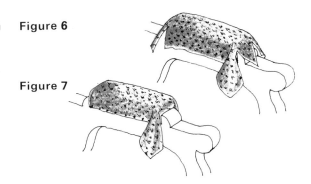

Figure 7

Figure 8

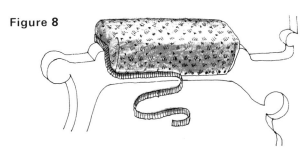

Figure 9

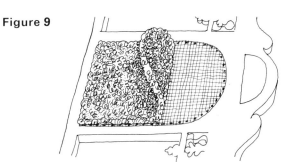

Figure 10

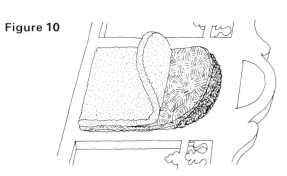

Figure 11

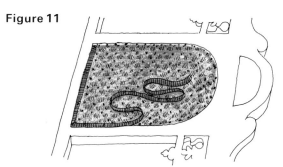

Project 6
Square armchair

Introduction

An upholstered armchair is much larger and more complicated than any of the projects described so far and you should have tackled at least one or two of these, including the sprung dining chair, before you proceed with this one. Allow yourself plenty of time and make sure you have a large, clear work area which can be left in disarray until the chair is finished.

Following the steps outlined in project 2, remove all the layers of old upholstery until you are left with the frame. As with the smaller projects, keep all the old layers so you can refer to their structure as you work, and use them to help you estimate the number of springs and the amount of padding and covering fabric you will need. Your chair may, of course, be larger or smaller than this one, so quantities and sizes may differ.

You will find a piece of cane (or occasionally metal) bent in a broad U shape supporting the structure of the seat at the front. If this is not broken, you can reuse it; otherwise you will have to make a new one from a piece of ordinary garden cane. To do this, measure the total length of the old cane and cut a new piece to this length. Bend it by carving a V-shaped nick halfway through the diameter at the appropriate points and pressing the two halves of each nick together to form a right angle.

You will notice that at each part of the chair (arms, seat and back) the final covering fabric is attached before you proceed to the next. This is because the rails to which you attach the cover become inaccessible when you put on the padding at the next stage. The arms are always done first.

Although it is fitted, the cover of this chair is constructed much like a loose cover, that is, in parts which are completed separately, then fixed in place.

Tools

scissors
pencil
tape-measure
hammer
webbing stretcher
springing needle
pins
skewers
double bayonet needle
tailor's chalk
regulator needle
slipping needle

Materials

black and white (first-quality) webbing: see project 2, figure 3 for measurements and add 500 mm (20 in)

20 mm ($\frac{5}{8}$) improved tacks, 13 mm ($\frac{1}{2}$) fine tacks

340 g (12 oz) hessian — enough to cover the arm frames, the seat over the springs (see figure 26) and the chair back (front and back)

linter felt — small pieces for front arm pads and filling in hollows, one large piece for covering the seat and front panel and one piece for covering the front panel

D7 polyether foam — two pieces the size of the tops of arms but 25 mm (1 in) longer

contact adhesive

twine (upholsterer's twine is always sold by the reel)

horsehair — use the old stuffing to gauge approximately how much you need

sheet (skin) wadding — enough to cover the inside and top arms, over the padding

60 g (2 oz) Courtelle — enough to cover the inside arms, the seat and front panel (see figure 46), and the back (front, back and top rail)

covering fabric — enough to go over all surfaces of the padded chair and attach to the frame, and to make the seat cushion piping cord — enough to pipe the seams, as shown in the diagram of the covered chair overleaf

springs: we used twelve 225 mm (9 in) gauge 9 and five 130 mm (5 in) gauge 10 springs for the seat, and six 150 mm (6 in) gauge 12 and three 125 mm (5 in) gauge 10 springs for the back

galvanized staples

cane for the seat front — use the one you removed with the old upholstery if you can (see figure 25) or make a new one from a length of garden cane (see introduction)

sticky tape

laid cord

ginger fibre for padding the back and round the seat springs — use the old stuffing to estimate quantities

25 mm (1 in) thick rubberized hair — a piece large enough to go over the seat (see figure 37) and a piece for the inside of the chair back (see figure 59)

40 mm (1½ in) curtain heading tape the width of the seat from arm to arm, plus 300 mm (12 in)

tack or tape roll long enough to go round the sides and across the top of the chair back (see figure 56)

cushion of Dacron-covered foam (see project 1, figures 31 & 32) or feathers to fit the chair seat

Figures 1–19 The arms

Reupholstering this type of chair begins with the arms, because once the seat is in place, the bottom rails to which you anchor the arm padding and cover are virtually inaccessible.

The diagram on the right shows the names of each section. Repeat all the following instructions for the second arm.

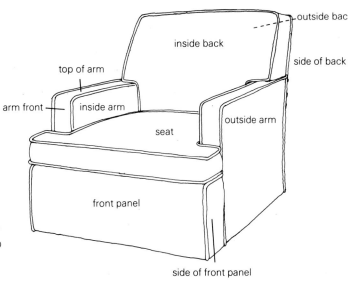

Figure 1 Attaching the webbing and hessian

Attach several strips of webbing to the arm frame on the inside, about three fixed vertically and two horizontally. Detailed instructions for attaching webbing are given in project 2, figures 3–8.

Cut a piece of 340 g (12 oz) hessian about 25 mm (1 in) larger all round than the arm frame. Temporarily tack it over the inside of the frame (**1**). Make sure the hessian is smooth and taut, then drive the tacks home. Now turn up a 13 mm (½ in) hem all round and tack it down, placing the tacks between those already in position under the hem.

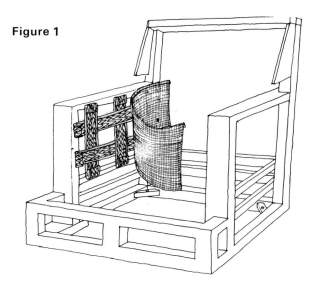

Figure 1

Figures 2–8 Putting on the padding

In order to soften the front edge of each arm, roll up a little linter felt or Courtelle lengthways in a piece of webbing the same length as the arm is wide. Tack this, rolled edge forward, slightly over the front of the arm frame (**2** and **3**).

Figure 2

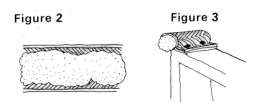

Figure 3

Figure 4

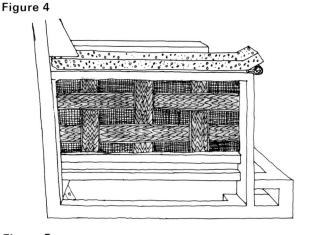

Cut a piece of 40 mm (1½ in) thick D7 polyether foam the same width as the top of the arm and 25 mm (1 in) longer. (Use a very sharp trimming or kitchen knife, or one with a serrated blade, or ask the foam retailer to cut it for you.) Glue this piece to the top of the arm by applying a layer of contact adhesive, then pressing the foam in place firmly, sliding it under the side pieces attached to the back frame, as shown (**4**). Fold the end of the foam down over the rolled edge at the front of the arm so that the top edge of the foam is butted against the front of the arm frame (**5**). Tack or staple in place, to form a smooth, curved edge.

Figure 5

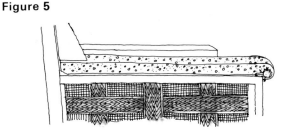

With a springing needle and twine, make bridle ties on the hessian on the inside of the arm in the pattern shown (figure 6). For full instructions, see project 2, figures 12–14. Take a handful of horsehair, tease it out with your fingers and insert it under and around the ties (**6**), blending the handfuls together and adding more until you have a firm, smooth, even layer of hair about 25 mm (1 in) thick. The horsehair should cover only the hollow area in the centre of the inside arm and not the frame itself.

Figure 6

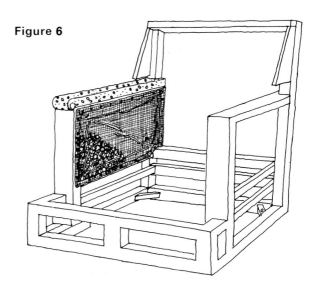

Cut a piece of skin wadding about 25 mm (1 in) larger all round than the inside arm frame plus enough to go over the foam along the top of the arm. Staple or tack it to the frame all round (**7**), then trim it to the frame as closely as possible, fitting it round the back frame as shown in figure 7.

Cut a piece of 60 g (2 oz) Courtelle large enough to cover the inside arm and attach it to the outside frame as shown in figure 8. Staple or tack it in position in the usual way, cutting and/ or folding at the corners and trimming where necessary (**8**).

Figures 9–17 Putting on the arm covers

Figure 7

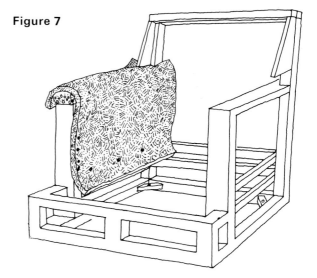

Measure and cut a piece of your covering fabric 25 mm (1 in) wider than the width across the top and front of the arm, and about 150 mm (6 in) longer, centring the pattern if necessary. Now measure and cut a piece of covering fabric 75 mm (3 in) longer and wider than the outside of the arm frame, and another for the inside, taking these inside measurements from the top of the arm to the bottom of the topmost side rail, where you attached the hessian (see figure 9). Lay the appropriate piece of fabric in position along the top of the arm and down the front. Cut a small nick into both sides of this piece, at the point where the top of the arm becomes the front (**9**).

Figure 8

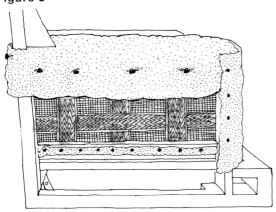

Figure 9

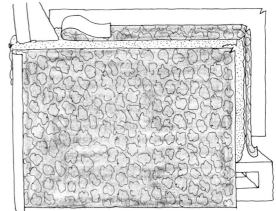

Project 6

Cut diagonal strips of fabric and make a long length of piping as explained in project 1, figures 21–25. The amount you need depends on the sum of all the measurements of the seams to be piped. It is best to make the piping in several long pieces, since it is difficult to join lengths of piping together once it has been made up.

Right sides together, pin a strip of piping to each side of the central arm strip, then sew the inside and outside pieces to this strip, folding the strip at the nicks so that they fall at the front corners of the side pieces (**10**).

Turn the arm cover right side out and place it in position, anchoring it with one temporary tack at the back of the top arm strip. Pull it taut towards the front and temporarily tack it to the bottom of the front arm panel at each side (**11**).

Pull the inner arm fabric towards the back and anchor it at the back with another temporary tack. Repeat for the outside arm.

Make a cut just inside and parallel to the piping, from the top of the back towards the front until you reach the frontmost edge of the back rail, as shown in figure 12. Remove the inside temporary tack (**12**).

At the other side of the back rail, make a second parallel cut in the fabric, again as far as the front edge of the back rail. Pull the fabric firmly to the back round the rail and temporarily tack it (**13**).

Figure 10

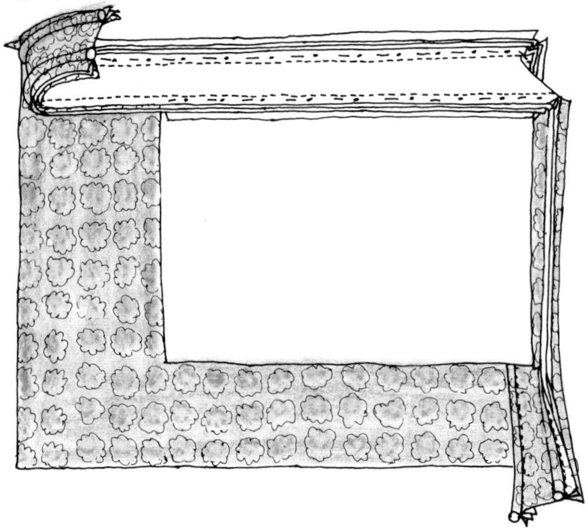

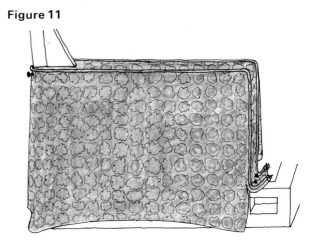

Figure 11

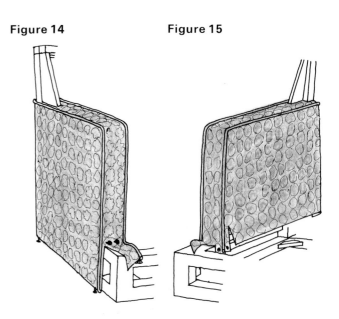

Figure 12   **Figure 13**

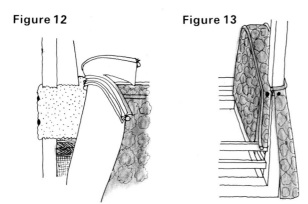

At the bottom of the front of the arm, make a cut inside and parallel to the piping up to the point where the front arm forms a right angle with the top of the front panel. Remove the temporary tack from here. Pull the fabric firmly down at the front of the outside arm cover and temporarily tack it under the bottom rail (**14**).

Make another cut inside the piping at the other side of the front of the arm, remove the other temporary tack, pull the fabric down and anchor with another temporary tack to the inside of the arm at the bottom (see figure 15).

Figure 14   **Figure 15**

From the bottom inside front of the arm, make a diagonal cut up to the bottom inside corner of the side rail. Anchor with a temporary tack as shown (**15**). Remove the temporary tack at the outside back and pull the inside fabric under the rail and through to the outside (**16**).

Figure 16

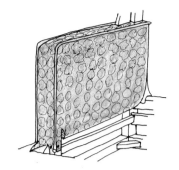

Lift up the outside arm cover and fasten it out of the way. Temporarily tack down the inside arm cover you have pulled through to the outside face of the rail (**17**).

Figure 17

Remove the temporary tack holding the inside arm cover to the back of the arm rail. Smooth the cover down and towards the back until it feels smooth and taut, and put another temporary tack inside the back rail to hold it in place. Trim and tack the fabric neatly round the lower back rail. There is no more to be done to the arm covers until the chair has reached a further stage.

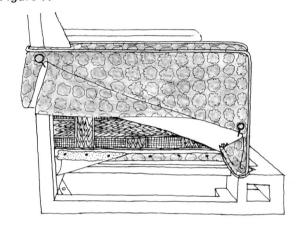

Figures 18–54 The seat

These instructions refer to a seat with a cushion which rests on top of the springs and padding.

Figure 18 Attaching the webbing

Tack strips of webbing to the underside of the frame as described in project 2, figures 3–8. The strips should be no more than their own width apart and attached in a woven pattern (**18**).

Figure 18

Figures 19 & 20 Attaching and lashing the main seat springs

For an average-size chair, you will need twelve 250 mm (9 in) gauge 9 springs spaced in three rows of four across the seat, with a gap between the front edge and the first row of springs as shown in figure 18. Lay them on the webbing, making sure that all the knots in the tops of the springs are facing away from the frame to prevent them wearing through the hessian which will be stretched over them. Attach each spring to the webbing in three places in the same way as explained in project 4, figures 2–5 (and shown in figure 18). Begin with the middle row, then do the front row, then the back row.

To lash the springs to the frame, first drive in temporary tacks along the bottom back rail, aligning each with the centre of each row of springs. Cut four pieces of laid cord twice as long as the frame is deep. Leaving a loose end of at least 30 cm (12 in), knot each length of cord around one of the tacks, then drive it home.

Project 6

Now lash the springs to the frame in much the same way as described in project 4, figures 6–12; only the position of the knots varies slightly. The first knot is made at the waist of the first spring in each row. The second is made at the top of the same spring, in a straight line toward the front. The second spring is lashed twice at the top only, continuing the straight line, and the front spring is lashed first at the top, then at the waist. Drive in a row of similarly positioned tacks along the bottom front rail, then anchor the pieces of cord to them in the same way (**19**).

Now use the lengths of cord left over at both ends to knot round the top of the springs at the front and back respectively, near the frame. Pull on this cord so the back springs lean very slightly towards the back rail and the front ones towards the front (**20**). Repeat this lashing from side to side so that the side rows of springs lean toward the nearest rails and the four corner springs lean slightly toward their corners.

Figures 21–25 The front rail springs

You will need some 130 mm (5 in) gauge 10 springs to go on the top of the front rail. Making sure the knots are in the correct position as shown in figure 21, space these springs evenly along the rail, against the front edge, and anchor each one with two or three galvanized staples round the bottom coil (see figure 21). If you are using an electric staple gun, two staples on each spring will hold them.

Cut a strip of webbing about 104 mm (4 in) longer than the front rail and lay it on the rail over the bottom coils of the springs. Tack or staple it in position round the inside and outside of each spring and at the two ends of the rail (**21**).

To lash these springs, cut a piece of laid cord one and a half times the length of the front rail. Drive a temporary tack into the top of the rail at one end, knot the cord around it tightly and drive the tack home. Drive in one temporary tack between each spring but towards the front edge of the rail, and one at the other end of the rail. Make a knot around the waist of the first spring, then pull the cord so the spring leans forward. Knot the cord around the next temporary tack and drive it home. Continue in this way until all the springs have been lashed and are leaning toward the front (**22**). It is very important that the springs remain level with one another, so when you have lashed each one, push it back to an upright position and check that it is the same height as its neighbours. Knot the cord around the last tack, drive it home, then trim the cord.

Figure 19

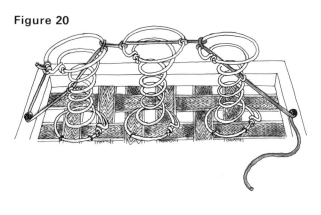

Figure 20

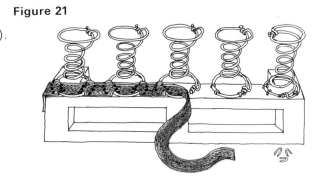

Figure 21

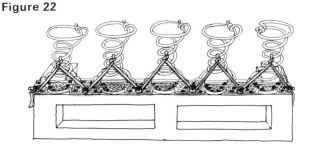

Figure 22

Cut a piece of twine about 1.25 m (4 ft) long and double it. You will need as many of these double lengths as there are front springs (five for this chair). Put a temporary tack into the front of the rail at the centre of each spring. At each spring, loop the twine round the bottom of the spring at the back, then round the waist of the spring as shown in figure 23. Take the twine to the top coil and loop round the back and front of the spring. This process involves three kinds of loops so study the diagram carefully. Making sure your spring is standing straight up and level with its neighbours, pull the twine down to the front of the rail, loop it around the temporary tack, and drive the tack home (**23**). Lash all the springs in this way and trim the twine.

Cut a single piece of twine twice the length of the front rail. Drive a temporary tack into one end of the front rail as shown in figure 24. Lash the first spring at the waist and top, then at the existing lashing, then at the other side. Continue along the row, lashing at the tops of the springs and at the cord in the middle of each, and anchoring at the other side in the usual way (**24**).

Take the piece of cane (or metal) which you removed from the top of the springs when you stripped off the old upholstery. Put it back in position and tape it temporarily to the springs, as shown in figure 25. To lash the cane, cut eleven pieces of twine each about 1.25 m (4 ft) long. Double one of these lengths and lash the cane to one spring with a loop like a blanket stitch, but made without a needle. Continue making these on the same spring until your twine is used up and there is a 26 mm (1 in) area of lashing.

detail of the blanket-stitch lashing shown in figure 25

Knot the twine to finish. Lash all the springs to the cane in this way, then lash again at each end of the cane rail, at the back of the end springs and at the ends of the cane, as shown (**25**).

Figures 26-34 Attaching the hessian

Measure and cut a piece of hessian large enough to go from the back of the seat, over the springs (and down between the main springs and the front springs) to under the bottom front rail, and from under one side rail, over the springs and under the opposite side rail, allowing for a 25 mm (1 in) hem all around. Turn under a hem and temporarily tack the hessian along the top of the bottom back rail (**26**); tacks can be 75–100 mm (3–4 in) apart.

Figure 23

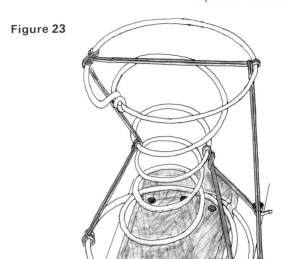

Figure 24

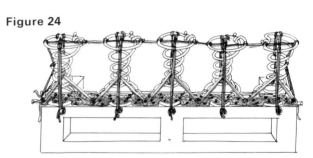

Figure 25

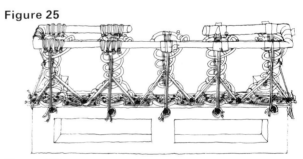

Figure 26

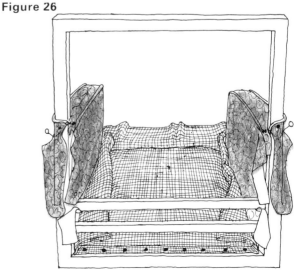

Project 6

Pull the hessian forward and tuck it down to make a gully between the main sprung section and the front row of springs. To anchor this in position, cut a small hole in the hessian at each inside front corner of the bottom front rail (at the bottom of the gully), and put in a temporary tack at each side of the bottom rail at the nearest point. Now cut a piece of laid cord slightly longer than the front rail and knot it around one temporary tack. Drive the tack home, pass the cord through the first hole, across the tucked-in section of the hessian as in the cross-section (**27**), through the other hole, knot it round the other temporary tack, and drive the tack home.

Cut into the hessian at the front corners and tuck the excess down the sides between the springs and the side rails.

Fold back the hessian at the front over the seat as shown in the cross-section (**28**). Cut a second piece of laid cord double the length of the front rail and thread it on to a springing needle. Put in temporary tacks across the top of the bottom front rail, about 100 mm (4 in) apart (see figure 29). Knot one end of the cord round one of the tacks and drive it home. With your needle, stitch the hessian, catching the strip of laid cord previously attached, anchoring each stitch to one of the tacks just inserted (**29**) and driving it home. Finish off with an anchoring tack.

Fold the hessian back over the front springs so that it hangs over the front rail and between the front springs and the front of the arms (**30**). Pull the hessian down gently to the centre of the bottom front rail and put in a temporary tack. Add more temporary tacks all along this front rail about 75 mm (3 in) apart, making sure that the hessian is smooth and straight. If necessary, trim the hessian at the front to about 50 mm (2 in) from the tacks.

Pull the hessian down over the sides of the bottom front rail, folding it neatly over the corners, and anchor with temporary tacks, two at the bottom and one halfway up (**31**). Trim the hessian close to these tacks.

Figure 27

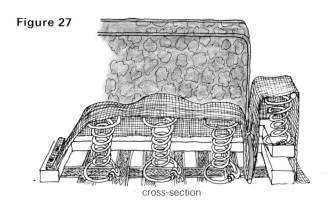

cross-section

Figure 28

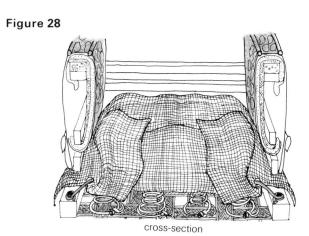

cross-section

Figure 29

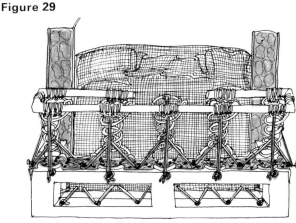

Figure 30

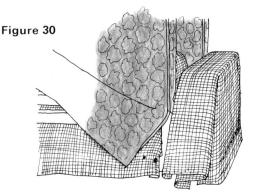

Figure 31

Thread your springing needle with twine and use a large blanket stitch to sew down the front edges as far as the upper rail, making them neat as shown in figure 32. Still with a springing needle and twine, anchor the hessian to the cane and front springs with a continuous line of blanket stitches round the cane (**32** and **33**).

Pull the hessian down between the main seat springs and the side rails. Anchor with a line of temporary tacks, cutting and folding the hessian at the back corners for neatness. With a springing needle and twine, stitch the main seat springs to the hessian as described in project 4, figure 18. Now stitch the front springs to the hessian in the same way, in the pattern shown (figure 34). To stop the edge springs separating from the main ones when the chair is sat on, cut a piece of laid cord about 1.25 m (4 ft) long, thread it on to a springing needle and sew each front main spring to its nearest edge spring, pulling them together (**34**). Finish with a simple knot.

Figure 32

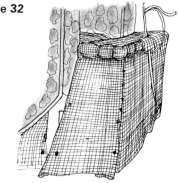

Figure 33

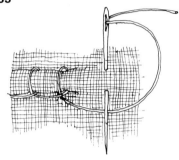

Figure 34

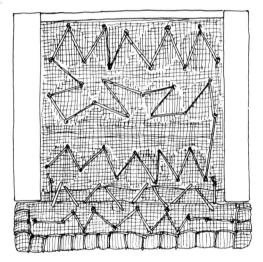

Figures 35-39 Putting on the padding

Take handfuls of ginger fibre and stuff them down between the edge springs and the main springs until the fibre feels firm and fits nicely under the stitches you have just made (**35**).

Remove the temporary tacks along the bottom back rail of the chair, pull the hessian taut and drive in permanent tacks more closely spaced; say 25 mm (1 in) apart. Do the same along the side rails and trim the hessian (figure 36). Tack around the back corners neatly. Remove the temporary tacks along the bottom front rail, pull the hessian taut, and add more tacks. Remove the temporary tacks from the folded hessian at the sides of the front rail, pull it taut and tack it down to the upper rails as shown (**36**). Trim.

Figure 35

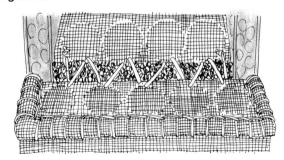

Figure 36

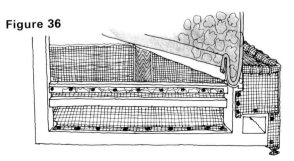

With large, sharp scissors, cut a piece of 25 mm
(1 in) thick rubberized hair wide enough to go
over the springs and reach the bottom rails on
each side, and long enough to reach from the
top of the bottom back rail to about 75 mm (3 in)
beyond the front edge of the chair. Place it in
position and make straight cuts into the corners
so that you can tuck the side and back edges
into place on their respective rails (**37**). The hair
should not be tucked directly on top of the
hessian, but over the rail above the bottom one.
If there are any hollow places between the main
springs and the front edge ones, lift up the
rubberized hair and tuck in a little more fibre.

Fold under the front edge of the hair so it is flush
with the front edge of the springs, and anchor it
temporarily with upholstery skewers (or sharp
kitchen ones) (**38**). Trim the corners so they
fold under neatly then fold under the side edges,
anchoring with skewers. Tuck the excess hair
down between the edge springs and the front of
the arms. Cut a piece of laid cord one and a half
times the length of the front rail, then drive in a
temporary tack on the bottom side rail as shown
in figure 38. Anchor the cord to the tack, pull it
taut so that it goes under the arm and across the
seat to the other arm, then anchor it at the other
side in the same way (see figure 38).

Cut a piece of twine about 3 m (10 ft) long and
thread a double bayonet needle. Sew a row of
top stitches around the front edge of the seat as
shown (**39**), through the hessian (below the
cane) and the rubberized hair. Instructions for
this stitch are in project 3, figures 25–28.
Remove the skewers as you go.

In order to build up the sides of the main sprung
area so they are tight against the arms, stuff
some ginger fibre up between the rubberized
hair and the hessian. You should not now be
able to get your hand down the side of the seat.
Do the same at the back so that the hair is right
against the rail.

Anchor the rubberized hair to the top of the
bottom side rails with temporary tacks which
need be only about 150 mm (6 in) apart.

To anchor the hair to the hessian and springs,
thread a double bayonet needle with twine, push
the needle into the hair about 100 mm (4 in)
from one corner, pull it almost all the way out at
the bottom, re-angle it slightly and push it out at
the top, catching the hessian and springs inside.
Make three stitches like this along each side
until you are back where you started, then move
into the centre and make a stitch there (see
figure 39 for pattern of stitches).

Figure 37

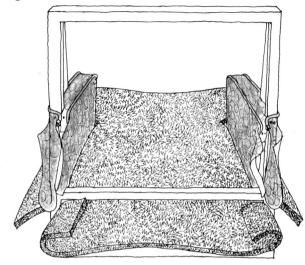

Figure 38

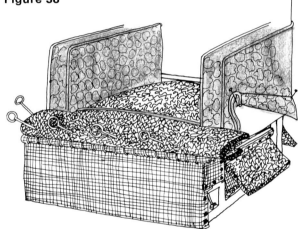

Figure 39

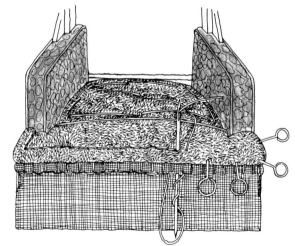

Figures 40–54 Putting on the seat cover

Cut a piece of covering fabric to cover the seat from below the front bottom rail to the first rail from the bottom at the back, and from one bottom side rail to the other. Lay this fabric in place and temporarily tack it to both ends of the bottom front rail. Trim the fabric to about 13 mm (½ in) from the tacks along the bottom, and also up the side and top edges of the seat front until you reach the inside of the arms. Make a small nick at each side to indicate where the front edge of the seat comes (see figure 40). Now make two cuts at the inside front corners (**40**) and tuck the fabric in neatly round the corners of the arms and down to anchor it temporarily.

Cut out two pieces of fabric about 300 mm (12 in) wider than the sides of the front edge panel and about 150 mm (6 in) deeper (**41**).

Attach a length of piping to both sides of the front panel section up to where it comes in front of the arms (**42**). Sew the side panels to the front of the main seat section (**43**), then along the top, forming a box shape and leaving the excess width at the back of this panel to tuck in.

Put the covering fabric in place on the seat and mark a line across the underside of the material with chalk about 175 mm (7 in) in from the front edge, from the front of one arm to the front of the other. Sew a length of 40 mm (1½ in) curtain heading tape to the underside of the fabric along this line, leaving about 150 mm (6 in) free at both ends (**44**).

Figure 40

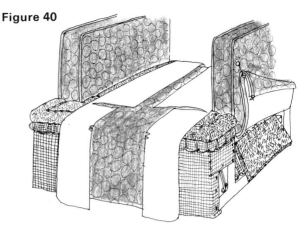

Figure 41

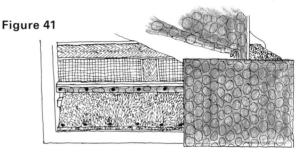

Figure 42

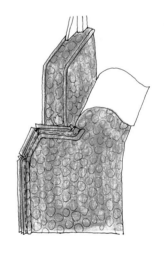

Figure 43

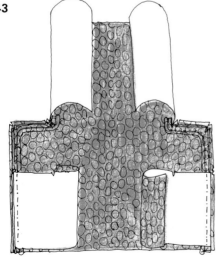

Figure 44

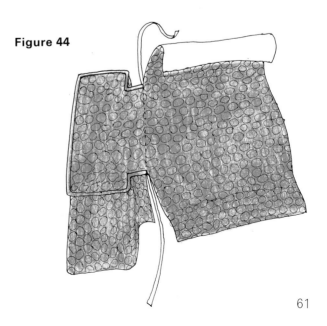

Put the cover back on the seat neatly and pull it into place. Take the ends of the tape, push them down over the hair and pull them through under the arms to the outside. Pull on these tapes gently so the cover fits smoothly over the top of the seat, then anchor the ends of the tape to the bottom rail with tacks in the usual way. Anchor the cover to the seat along the tape line with long pins and fold the seat cover back from the front so the edge of the tape is exposed (see figure 45).

Figure 45

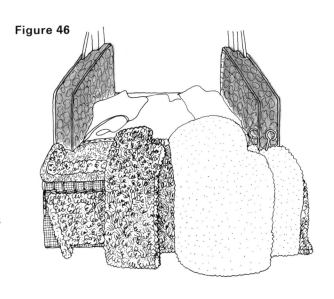

Thread a double bayonet needle with a piece of twine two and a half times as long as the width of the seat at the front, and knot one end. Now sew the seat cover to the seat itself by means of long running stitches along the tape: beginning at one side of the seat, put your needle down into the tape, through the seat, until the point comes out underneath. Then angle the needle towards the centre of the chair and push it out 40 mm (1½ in) from the point where you went in . Continue making these stitches along the tape, pull them taut, and knot to finish (**45**).

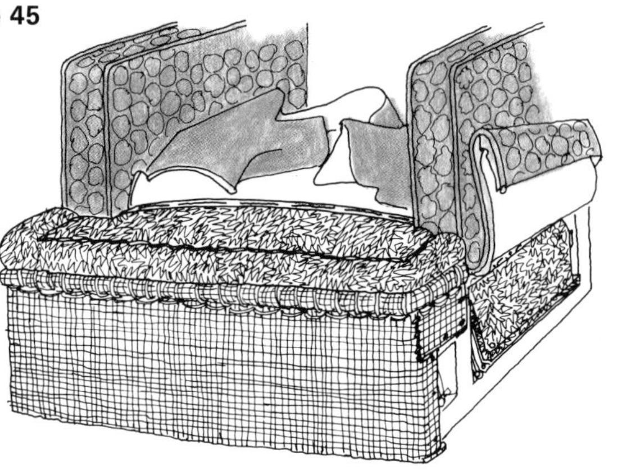

Tear off small pieces of linter felt and place them on top of the rubberized hair along the front edge, to fill in the hollow formed by the top stitches, as shown in figure 46. Now cut a piece of linter felt large enough to cover this front panel and go just over the front edge. Cut another piece of linter felt wide enough to cover the front edge panel from side to side and long enough to reach from the tape line, over the edge, to the bottom of the chair (see figure 46). Press this in place; it is not necessary to fasten it down.

Figure 46

Cut a piece of Courtelle about 150 mm (6 in) larger all round than the second piece of linter felt. Lay it over the felt and anchor it in place along the tape line with skewers, as shown (**46**). Pull the Courtelle down at the front and tack or staple it along the bottom front edge of the chair. Trim as closely as possible.

At the sides of the front edge panel, pad the gaps with pieces of linter felt, then lay over one large piece as you did at the top (**47**). Pull the Courtelle down from the top, beyond the felt slightly, then cut it diagonally, trim and fold over from the front (**48**). Tack the Courtelle into place and trim (**49**).

Figure 47

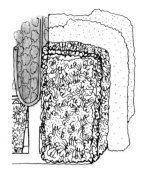

Figure 48

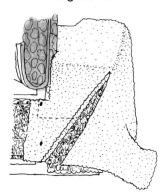

Figure 49

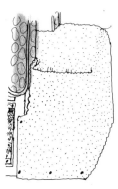

Pull the covering fabric into position over the Courtelle and check for fit.

Lift up one inside corner, near the front of the arms, make a diagonal cut into it from the raw edge, and extend it bit by bit so you can pull the front sides of the cover neatly down between the front edge panel and the front of the arm. Repeat on the other side (**50**).

Pull the finished cover down into place at the front and temporarily tack it under the centre of the front rail. Put in more temporary tacks along this rail (see figure 51).

Fold the rear half of the seat cover to the front at the tape line (see figure 51). Cut a piece of linter felt large enough to cover the top of the seat from tape to back, and be tucked in slightly all around. Lay this on the seat, then cut a piece of Courtelle the same size and lay it on the top (**51**).

Fold the seat cover back over these layers and tuck it down at the sides and back so you can pull it through the rails from the outside, cutting and folding at the corners where necessary. Tack this fabric down with a few temporary tacks along the bottom rail at the sides and back (**52**).

Check that the front of the chair is now the same height on both sides. If one side is slightly higher, adjust it by removing the temporary tacks under the side panel pieces, pulling the cover down firmly to compress the filling, and re-tacking it.

Make a slightly angled cut into the fabric from below, from the back edge of the side front panel to the point where the two rails meet (**53**). It is better to make your cut slightly too short and extend it with tiny cuts around the area until you can push the cover down neatly between the front section and the arm. The blunt end of a regulator needle will help you with this tricky process.

The bottom section of fabric can be simply pulled toward the back and stapled or tacked. Release the fabric covering the outside arm so its piping falls down over the side panels you have just been working on. Slip-stitch the two covering sections together (**54**), or use a thin line of suitable adhesive.

If you are satisfied with the front section of your chair, drive home the tacks underneath the bottom rail.

Figure 50

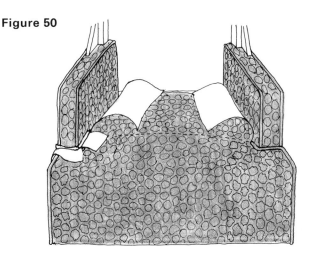

Figure 51

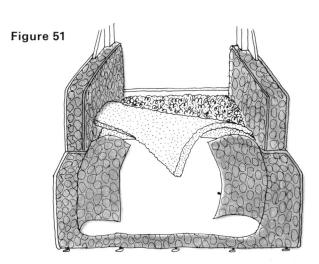

Figure 52

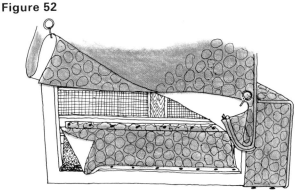

Figure 53   **Figure 54**

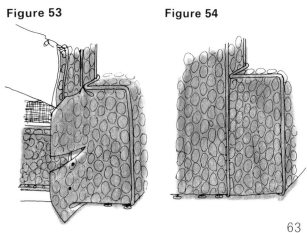

Project 6

Figures 55–72 The back

Figure 55 Attaching the webbing

Attach three rows of webbing horizontally and
three vertically to the back of the frame, arranged
in a woven pattern as usual. Leave the tacks as
temporary ones, however, since you may have to
remove them later to fix the back and seat fabric.
These strips of webbing should be at right angles
to each other and in straight rows, even if the
back frame is wider at the top. Tack the vertical
rows of webbing to the top face of the top rail.

Figures 55 & 56 Attaching and lashing the springs

You will need six springs of one size and three of
a slightly smaller size. The larger ones should be
placed in two rows of three at the top and centre
of the back and the smaller springs in a single
row at the bottom, since more pressure will be
exerted at the top. The larger of these sizes
should project slightly beyond the frame of your
chair; the smaller should be about level with it.
For this chair, we used six 156 mm (6 in) gauge
12 springs and three 130 mm (5 in) gauge 10
ones. Tip the chair so it is lying flat on its back
with the top rail nearest you. Position the springs
with all the knots possible at the one o'clock
position, as explained for the seat springing.

Figure 55

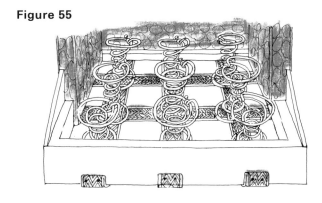

With a springing needle and twine, attach these
springs to the webbing as for the seat (**55**).

Cut a 2 m (6 ft 6 in) length of twine and double
it; treat this as if it were one piece of twine. Put
in three temporary tacks across the top and
bottom rails, aligning with the centre of each
spring. Starting with the central spring farthest
away from you, loop the twine first around the
waist of the spring, then pull the twine to the
tack, bending the spring slightly toward the
bottom rail. Loop the twine around the tack and
drive it home. Now loop the twine around the
top of the spring at the back, go straight across
to the front and loop, then make two loops at
the back and front of the middle spring, and two
at the top of the spring nearest to you, back and
front again. Now pull the spring sharply forward,
more than you did at the bottom, loop the twine
around the tack and drive it home. Repeat this
for the rows of springs on each side of this one
as shown in figure 56, and then for the top two
horizontal rows, putting in only two tacks on
each side rail. The top two rows should be lashed
from the top of the side rails rather than from the
waist of the edge springs. It is not necessary to
lash the bottom row horizontally.

Figure 56

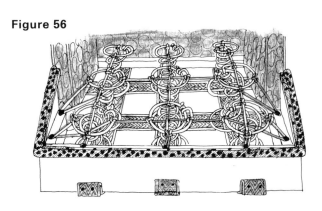

Cut three lengths of tack or tape roll long enough to go across the back and up the two sides of the back rail. Tack or staple this around the inside of the rail, mitring the corners (**56**).

Figure 57 Attaching the hessian

Cut a piece of hessian 150 mm (6 in) larger all around than the T-shape of the chair back. Tack this to the frame over the springs in the usual way. At the bottom of the back, pull the hessian down behind the seat to reach the rail, and tack. Tuck it in between the sides and the arms where there is no rail, cutting into the corners where necessary, and tack in position along the top and side rails, turning under a small hem. With a springing needle and twine, anchor the springs to the hessian in the usual way (**57**).

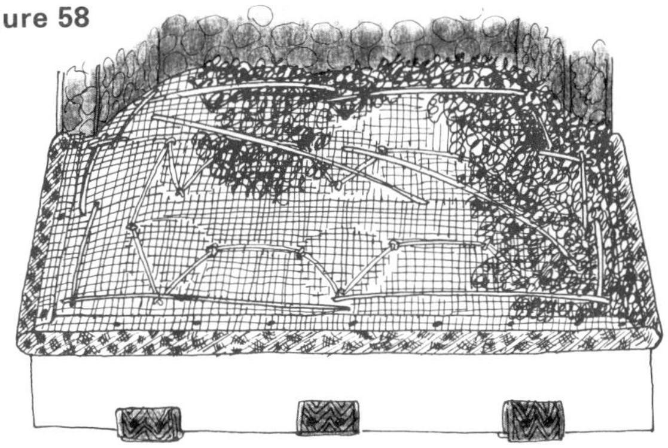

Figures 58-63 Putting on the padding

Again in the usual way, make bridle ties around and across the back in the pattern shown in figure 58. Stuff ginger fibre under and around the bridle ties, blending one handful with the next and adding more until it feels thick and firm (**58**). Tuck some more fibre down the sides by the arms to fill any gaps.

Cut a piece of rubberized hair 50 mm (2 in) larger all around than the shape of the chair back, including the arms (**59**). Place it in position and make straight cuts into the corners at the top of the arms so you can tuck the hair down between the back and the arms. Tack or staple it down around the top, inside the tack roll, and trim (**60**).

Tear off some pieces of linter felt and stuff them round the edge of the back to fill in the hollows where the tack roll meets the rubberized hair. Anchor the rubberized hair through the hessian and springs as you did with the seat, then cover the stitches with more linter felt (**61**).

Figure 57

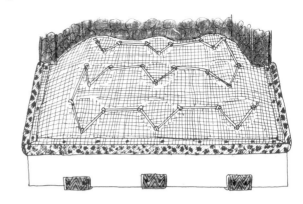

Figure 58

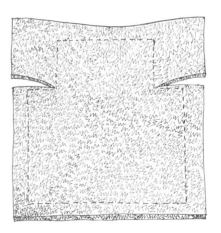

Figure 59

Figure 60

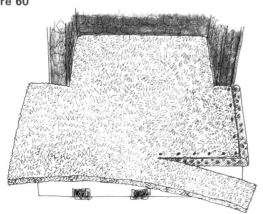

Figure 61

Project 6

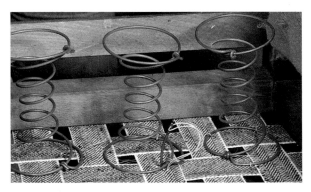

Attaching springs to webbing with twine.

Cut a piece of 40 mm (1½ in) Supersoft foam 75 mm (3 in) larger all around than the back and arms. Making cuts and nicks where necessary at the tops of the arms (**62**), tuck this down between the back and sides of the chair, over the rubberized hair. Pull the foam down over the top and sides of the back and anchor it with tacks to the top and side rails (**63**). Trim the foam with a sharp knife.

Cut a piece of Courtelle 150 mm (6 in) larger all around than your T-shape. Tuck it in around the bottom and the arms, tack it to the frame and sides in the usual way and trim.

Figures 64–70 Putting on the back cover

Cut a piece of covering fabric in a rectangle 100 mm (4 in) larger all round than the back, including the arms. Lay it in position and anchor it with skewers. Make horizontal cuts in from the sides at the top of the arms so the fabric fits around the top of the arms. Leaving a 13 mm (½ in) seam allowance, cut around the arms to make the fabric a T-shape, but try to leave a narrow piece at the bottom corners (as shown in figure 64) to use as a pull. Cut round the top and sides of the chair, again leaving a 13 mm (½ in) seam allowance. Sew piping round the top and sides of this piece, then sew a 150 mm (6 in) wide piece of any fabric or lining to the bottom for tucking in (**64**).

Figure 62

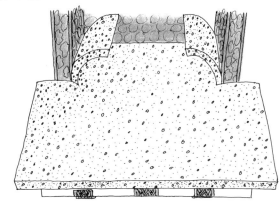

Figure 63

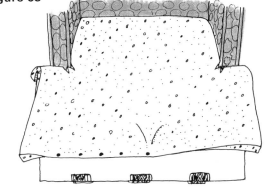

Figure 64

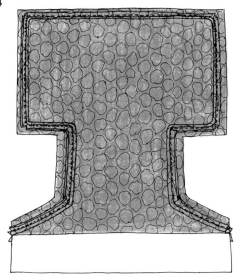

Figure 65

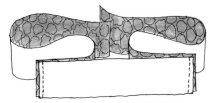

Cut three strips of fabric, each 13 mm ($\frac{1}{2}$ in) larger all around than the top and side borders of the chair back, all the way down to the seat at the sides for tucking in. Sew these together at what will be the top corners (**65**) and then sew this long border strip to the inside back cover along the piping edge. (If you wish, you can divide this border into two strips separated by piping to give the impression of a loose cushion, as shown in the picture on page 51.)

Put the cover in place on the chair, anchor it to the back of the frame with temporary tacks, and pull the excess fabric through to the back of the chair at the bottom (**66**).

At each corner, where the back meets the arms, pull the fabric out and make a cut to about 26 mm (1 in) away from the piping so the fabric can be spread out and tucked in neatly.

Pull the fabric down and make more cuts into it as shown so that it can be pulled down through the rails without puckering and tacked there (**67**).

Remove the temporary tacks from the top of the chair. Cut a piece of Courtelle large enough to cover the top rail without going over the edges, and push this into place along the rails, under the cover, paying particular attention to the corners. Temporarily tack the fabric down again, along the back of the top rail, as before (**68**).

Figure 66

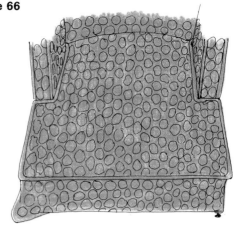

Figure 67

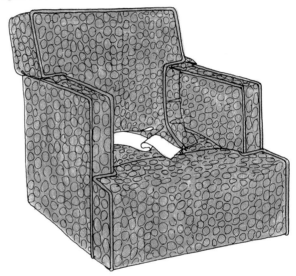

Figure 68

Pull the cover over the two sides of the chair back, above the arms, and anchor it to the back of the side rails with temporary tacks (**69**).

Make a cut into the fabric near the piping at the point where the side of the back meets the outside arm as shown. Pull the resulting flap of fabric through between the back and the arm to the back and anchor it with temporary tacks. Fold the remaining piece of fabric under, against the piping and temporarily tack it to the back of the rail (**70**). It may be necessary to undo the temporary tacks holding the back webbing in place in order to reach in and pull this fabric through. Repeat on the other arm.

Figure 69   **Figure 70**

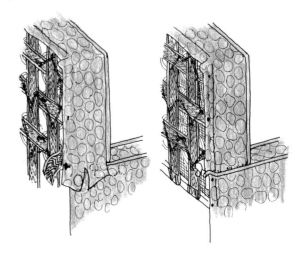

Project 6

Examine the top rail to make sure the cover is absolutely smooth and straight. If necessary, remove the temporary tacks and adjust the cover until you are satisfied with it. Drive the tacks home. Do the same along both sides of the back to the arms, trimming and folding neatly at the top two corners (see figure 71).

Figures 71–75 Finishing off

Check the temporary tacks holding the seat cover in place at the back, to see if the cover is straight. If it is not, adjust and trim any excess rubberized hair underneath before you tack or staple along the top face of the rail.

Do the same thing at each side, putting in tacks along the top face of the bottom rail. Trim and fold the fabric neatly at the corners.

You will have a lot of excess padding and fabric coming through to the back of the chair. Trim and tack it down where possible to make the back of your chair neat. Retack your webbing with permanent tacks.

Pull the outside arm covers down at each side so the fabric is straight, taut and smooth, making sure the piping along the arms falls in the right place. Temporarily tack it under the bottom side rails. Now pull this fabric toward the back of the chair, again so it is smooth, taut and straight, and temporarily tack it at the back faces of the vertical back rails. If you are satisfied with the look of the cover, drive the tacks home and trim the fabric (**71**).

Cut a piece of covering fabric 13 mm ($\frac{1}{2}$ in) larger all around than the back of the chair. Make a length of piping long enough to go along the top of it and down both sides, to the bottom of the chair. Place this fabric in position, fold under the top edge and pin it in place along the top of the chair, with the piping strip between this fabric and that which has already been attached, as shown (**72**). Slip-stitch in place along the top. Fold the cover out of the way over the front of the chair and tack the piping into place down the sides of the chair (**73**).

Cut a piece of hessian slightly larger than the back of the chair. Turn under a small hem and tack it permanently across the outside face of the top rail. Pull this hessian down so it is taut and firm over the back and tack it along the outside face of the bottom rail, then tack the sides, again making a hem. Trim all around (see figure 74).

Figure 71

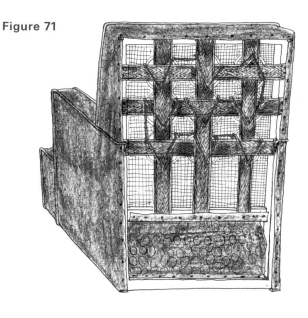

Figure 72

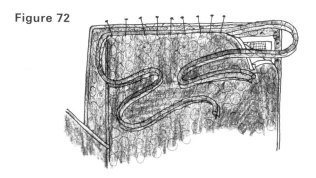

Figure 73

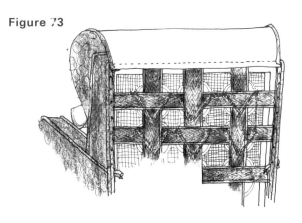

Cut a piece of Courtelle the same size as the back of your chair but long enough to fold under at the top and anchor it in position (**74**). Fold the covering fabric back into position, pull it straight and taut and temporarily tack it in place underneath the bottom rail. Trimming and folding neatly at the corners, turn the fabric under at the edges and slip-stitch it through the piping to the outside arm fabric with a slipping needle (**75**).

Turn the chair upside down, drive the tacks home underneath the back rail and trim the fabric. Cut a piece of black linen or hessian slightly larger than the base of the frame, turn under a small hem and tack it into place to cover your work.

Making the cushion cover

If the existing cushion is reusable, make a new cover for it by taking the old cover apart carefully and using it as a pattern to cut your covering fabric. If necessary, use the instructions for making piping and putting in a zip in project 1, figures 18–29.

If the cushion itself is too damaged to use, you will have to provide a new one, which should be made either of feathers or of best-quality rubber foam wrapped with Dacron as described in project 1, figures 31 & 32. Cut a template the same size and shape as the chair seat.

If you are having a feather cushion made, mark on the template that this is the size you want the finished stuffed cushion to be and the pad will be made slightly larger so that it will look plump and firm inside the cover.

If you are using foam, have a specialized dealer cut it for you and explain to him that you want your pad to be the same size as the template so the cover will fit tightly.

When your pad arrives, use the same template to cut the fabric for your cover, leaving a 13mm ($\frac{1}{2}$ in) seam allowance all around and following the instructions in project 1, figures 16–32.

Figure 74

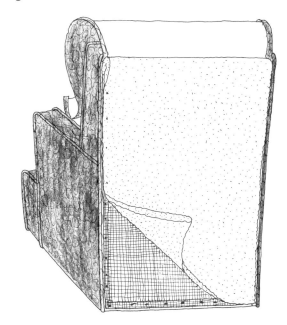

Figure 75

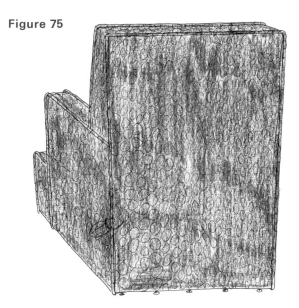

Project 7
Buttoned wing-chair

Introduction

There are many similarities between this project and the previous one so, before you begin, turn back and read the instructions for the square armchair. This armchair, however, differs from the other one, not only in the shape of the arms and back but also because it has no cushion on the seat, which must be built up with thicker padding. As with all the projects, you should begin this one by carefully stripping off the old upholstery and keeping it so that you can refer to it as you work. This process is particularly vital with buttoned furniture, since you will need the old back cover to give you the positions of the buttons on the new one. (Working out this positioning from scratch is not a job for the amateur; it is fairly tricky and really requires the skill of a master upholsterer.)

Because this chair is generally rounded, with few flat surfaces, the cover is applied in a different way from that in project 6 in that it is moulded round the curves and tacked directly on to the frame, rather than assembled in sections and then fitted over the padding. Because of this, a new technique called back-tacking is introduced which makes it possible to attach the final cover to awkward places so that no tacks are visible.

Tools

scissors

pencil or tailor's chalk

tape-measure

hammer

webbing stretcher

springing needle

regulator needle

double bayonet needle 450 mm (18 in) long

paper (for template)

pins, skewers

small slipping needle

Materials

black and white (first-quality) webbing: see project 2, figure 3 for measurements and add 500 mm (20 in)

20 mm ($\frac{5}{8}$ in) improved tacks

13 mm ($\frac{1}{2}$ in) fine tacks

340 g (12 oz) hessian — 12 pieces slightly larger than the arms (see figures 2–6), the seat, the wings, the back (front and back) and front panel

twine (upholsterer's twine is always sold by the reel)

ginger fibre for padding the arms, the wing rails, and round the seat springs — use the old stuffing to estimate quantities

horsehair — gauge approximately how much you need from the old stuffing

sheet (skin) wadding to cover the padded arms, wings, seat and back

60 g (2 oz) Courtelle — enough to cover the arms, back (front and back) and side sections, and front panel (optional)

piping cord — enough to go round the fronts of the scroll arms and along the front of the seat.

scrim — two pieces large enough to go over the wing rails (see figure 18), and two pieces about 150 mm (6 in) larger all round than the chair seat and chair back

covering fabric — enough to go over all surfaces of the padded chair and attach to the frame

springs — we used nine 350 mm (14 in) gauge 9 and four 175 mm (7 in) gauge 10 springs for the seat, and nine 125 mm (5 in) gauge 12 springs for the back

galvanized staples

laid cord

cane for the seat front: you will probably be able to use the piece you removed with the old upholstery

linter felt — a piece slightly larger than the top of the seat

slipping thread

back-tacking strip or strip of card, long enough to go along the outer back and wings, along the top rails

Project 7

Figures 1–15 The arms

See the diagram of the bare frame (**1**) for the names of different rails.

Figure 2 Attaching the webbing and hessian

Attach three strips of webbing vertically between the top arm rail and the one immediately below it, on the inside, as shown (see figure 2). Instructions for attaching webbing are given in project 2, figures 3–8. It may be necessary to angle the strip nearest the back so it is parallel with the back rail. Cut a piece of 340 g (12 oz) hessian slightly larger than the area contained within these rails. Turning over a small hem and starting in the middle of each side, tack or staple it along the inside of the top, bottom and front rails of this section, pulling it taut as you go. At the back, leave an opening of about 25–40 mm (1–1½ in) between the hessian and the back rail as shown in figure 2. Later on you will need to tuck in and anchor various layers here.

Figures 2–6 Attaching the first layer of padding

Beginning at one inner corner, make bridle ties with twine in a criss-cross pattern across this area as shown (see figure 2). Instructions for making bridle ties are given in project 2, figures 12–14. Now cut a piece of twine slightly longer than the top arm rail and anchor it by driving in a temporary tack at the back of the arm rail, knotting one end of the twine, looping it around the tack and driving the tack home. Pull the twine to the front of the rail and anchor it there in the same way (**2**).

Cut a piece of hessian about 150 mm (6 in) wider than the length of the arm and about two and a half times longer than the distance between the top rail and the one under it. Temporarily tack this down along the outside of the first arm rail from the top, leaving the hessian hanging down below the tacks (see figure 3). Take handfuls of ginger fibre and stuff them around the twine at the top of the arm (**3**), and around the bridle ties on the inner arm, blending one section into the next. Keep adding fibre until you have a firm, thick layer which extends to the back rail along the top and the inside of the arm. Push the hessian through to the inside of the chair, under the rail to which it is attached and pull it firmly over the top of the arm (**4**),

Figure 1

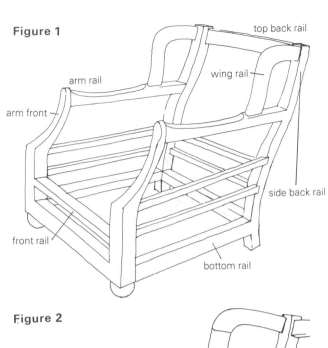

top back rail
wing rail
arm rail
arm front
side back rail
front rail
bottom rail

Figure 2

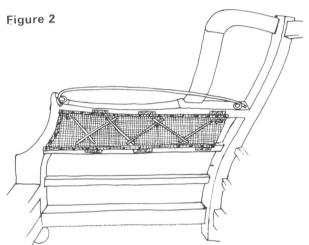

Figure 3

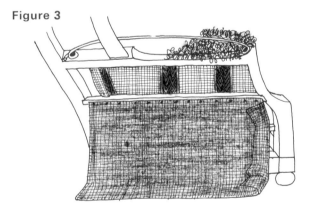

Figure 4

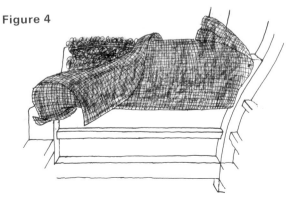

72

adjusting the fibre underneath as you go, and adding more if necessary. Pull the hessian firmly again and temporarily tack it to the outside of the top rail, first at the centre, then in a row along the arm as shown in figure 5, adjusting the fibre along the rail and teasing it into shape with the point of a regulator needle. Do not tack the hessian to the back rail, but leave a space there. To neaten the hessian round the back of the arm, cut into it and fold it around the front wing rail (**5**). Take out the temporary tacks to readjust the filling and hessian if necessary. Repeat these steps for the other arm.

At the front of each arm, stuff more fibre under the hessian to make a smooth, plump roll over the edge of the frame. Pull the hessian down from the top and across from both sides and anchor it with temporary tacks, always smoothing the surface, arranging or adding to the filling and teasing it forward as you go. Now remove these temporary tacks and turn the front edges of the hessian under around the scroll shape now formed, adjusting the fibre and trimming and folding where necessary. Now temporarily tack it into place at the inside front edge and around the top (**6**). To get the shape and finish right you may have to go over your work several times, taking out the tacks, adding to and arranging the fibre with a regulator, and pulling and folding the hessian.

Remove the temporary tacks from along the outside of the top arm rail. Tuck under this edge, pull the hessian straight and taut, replace the temporary tacks, check your work and drive the tacks home. Remove the temporary tacks holding the bottom edge of the hessian in place, pull it tight, and retack.

With twine and a double bayonet needle, make giant running stitches right through the hessian and the fibre across the inside of the arms (see figure 8) to hold these layers together.

Figures 7 & 8 Making blind and top stitches

Now make a row of blind stitches around the front of each arm in the position shown in figure 7. Detailed instructions for this stitch can be found in project 3, figures 18–24. While making these stitches, use your needle to pull the fibre towards the front to form a firm edge.

Following the same line, make a row of top stitches around the front of each arm (**7**), pulling the twine tight and teasing the fibre forward frequently, as before. See project 3, figures 25–28 for instructions on how to make

Figure 5

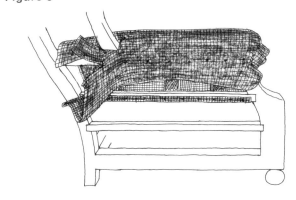

Figure 6

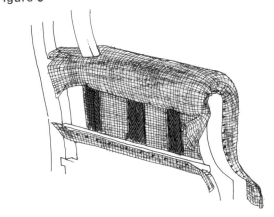

Figure 7

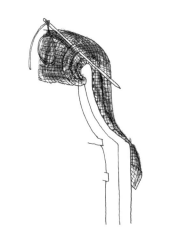

top stitches. This stitching will make a firmly anchored and clearly visible edge roll. The rows of blind stitches and top stitches should meet at the bottom of the padded section (see figure 8).

In order to make the padding along the outer arms firmer, make a row of top stitches along their top edge slightly larger than those at the front, to form a thick edge roll (**8**).

Figures 9 & 10 Adding the final padding

Turn the chair on its side. Take small pieces of horsehair and lay them in the gaps left by the stitching round the front of the arm, along the top, along the inside and underneath the arm (**9**) Lay a piece of sheet (skin) wadding over the work you have just done and tack it in place along the outside of the first rail from the top, where you first attached the hessian. Pull it smoothly under this rail, up over the padding and round to the outside again, anchoring it to the underside of the top arm rail (see figure 10). At the front, pull the wadding down over the edge and tack it round the front arm rail, pleating and cutting where necessary (**10**). Trim. Tack a small piece of wadding of the shape shown in figure 10 to the front of the arm.

At the back, cut, fold and trim the wadding so that it fits round the frame, then anchor it in exactly the same places as you did the hessian (see figures 5 and 6). Although not strictly necessary, you can cover this with a layer of Courtelle, attached in exactly the same way as the wadding, for an especially smooth finish.

Figures 11–15 Putting on the cover

Make a template of the front of the arm to the floor by tacking a piece of paper to the front section and drawing a line round the scroll shape from the back of the paper. Cut this shape out and use it as a pattern to cut a piece of covering fabric, leaving a 13 mm ($\frac{1}{2}$ in) seam allowance all round. Cut another piece of covering fabric about 50 mm (2 in) wider than the widest part of the inside arm and long enough to cover all the padded area over the arm. Anchoring it in place over the arm with skewers, cut the fabric round the front of the arm (**11**), again leaving a 13 mm ($\frac{1}{2}$ in) seam allowance. Press into position the piece of fabric you cut for the front and make a nick in both pieces at the top of the arm (**12**).

Make a length of piping (see project 1, figures 21–25) long enough to sew round the right side of the front fabric from under the curve, up

Figure 8

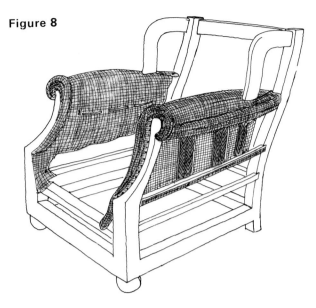

Figure 9

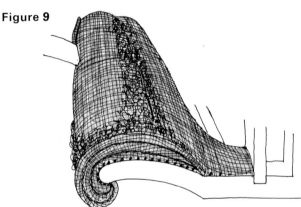

Figure 10

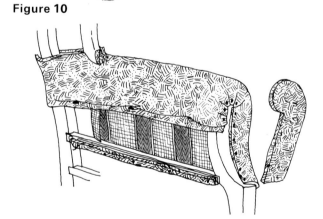

Figure 11

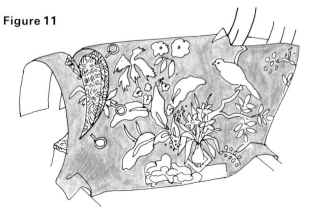

round the top, then down to where the chair's concave curve becomes the flat front, as shown in figure 13, leaving enough at each end to go down to the floor. At the curve of the fabric make small cuts into the seam allowance so the cover will fit neatly (**13**). Now sew the main piece of fabric to the front fabric, matching nicks.

Put the cover in place over the arm and temporarily tack it to the outside of the top arm rail, at the front facing and at the back rail, near the wing (**14**). Keep adjusting and retacking until the cover fits perfectly. At the rails, cut carefully into the fabric as shown in figure 15 so you can tack it round the wing and back rails at the top, and the back rail further down. Cut and tack similarly at the inside front so you can pull the bottom of the cover to the outside (**15**).

Figure 12

Figure 13   **Figure 14**   **Figure 15**

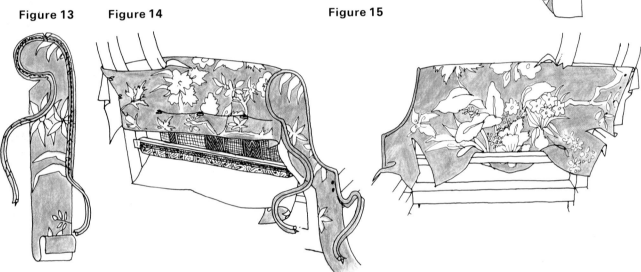

Figures 16–25 The wings

Figures 16 & 17 Attaching the webbing and hessian

In order to make the webbing especially strong, and also to save space, fold it in half lengthways and attach a single strip vertically to the inside of each wing frame at the back.

Cut a piece of hessian one and a half times larger than the wing area. Temporarily tack it to the wing, first along the inside front of the wing rail, pulling it between the webbing and the back rail, to the outside, cutting into the edges where necessary. Now temporarily tack it to the inside top of the rail (**16**). Now, at the outside of the wing, temporarily tack the remaining long edge along the inside face of the back rail (see figure 17). At the bottom of the wing, pull the hessian to the outside, cutting where necessary, and temporarily tack it to the top arm rail (**17**).

Figure 16   **Figure 17**

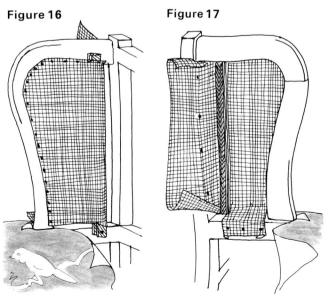

Project 7

Figures 18 & 19 Padding the wing rails

Cut a piece of scrim about 200 mm (8 in) longer than the whole wing rail and about 275 mm (11 in) wider. Turning under a small hem, temporarily tack this around the inner edge of the inside of the wing (**18**), so that the scrim hangs over the outside of the wing. You will have to make small pleats in the scrim around the curve.

Cut a piece of twine the same length as the scrim, for bridle ties. Put three temporary tacks inside the wing rail (as shown in figure 19), one at the top back, one at the top front and one at the bottom near the arm. Knot one end of your twine around this last tack, drive it home, then, leaving your twine loose, loop it around the second tack and drive it home. Loop it round the third tack and drive it home in the same way. Take large handfuls of ginger fibre and push them under and around the loops you have just made, blending the handfuls together (**19**).

Pull the scrim over the fibre and round to the other side of the rail. Keep adding fibre and working it in until you have a smooth, firm roll about 65 mm (2½ in) thick under the scrim, using your regulator needle to work the fibre into place. Turn under the scrim and temporarily tack it down at the top of the outside edge of the rail (see step 20). Keep checking the fibre as you tack, arranging it and adding more if necessary since this is how you form the basic shape of your wing. When you are satisfied that your roll is smooth, even and firm, drive these tacks home. Insert your regulator needle and ease the fibre towards the outside of the wing.

Figures 20 & 21 Making top stitches

Thread your double bayonet needle with twine and sew a row of top stitches around the outside edge of the rail as shown (**20**), starting from the bottom of the wing and constantly working the fibre toward the edge. Stop sewing a few centimetres from the end, but do not remove your needle and twine. Finish off this top end by neatening the fibre, adding more if necessary, trimming and folding the end of the scrim neatly and tacking it down (**21**). Continue

Figure 18

Figure 19

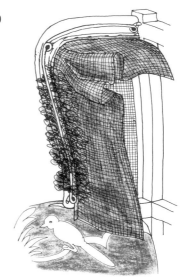

Figure 20

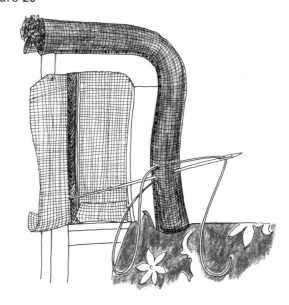

Figure 21

top stitching to the end of the wing and across the back of the wing rail. Drive home all the temporary tacks along the inside of the wing.

Figure 22

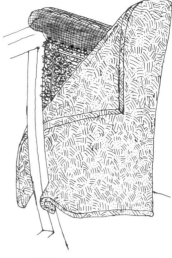

Figure 22 Padding the inside wing

Thread your springing needle with twine and make bridle ties across the inside of the wing. Tuck handfuls of horsehair under and around these ties in the usual way until the surface is smooth, thick and even. Add hair also along the edge roll and into the grooves made by the top stitching.

Cut a piece of skin wadding large enough to cover the inside of the wing and round to the outside of the roll (**22**). Tack it to the outside of the rail just beyond the scrim. Remove the temporary tacks holding the hessian to the back rail and push the wadding through in front of the back rail, as with the hessian. You will have to make cuts in the wadding so it will fold neatly around the rails (see figure 22). Cover this with a layer of Courtelle attached in the same way.

Figure 23

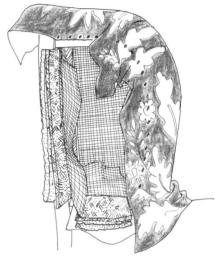

Figures 23–25 Putting on the cover

Measure the wing area covered by the hessian and padding and cut a piece of covering fabric about 250 mm (10 in) larger all around. Lay the fabric in place and temporarily tack it along the outside of the wing rail, easing it into gathers at the curves (**23**). Tuck the back edge of the cover through between the webbing and the back rail and fold under the lower edge above the arm (**24**). Temporarily tack it behind the back rail at the top, then pull the fabric firmly back from the side and temporarily tack it to the back rail (**25**). Where the wing meets the arm, you will have to make cuts in the fabric (see figure 24) so it will tuck neatly under the wing. Use your regulator needle to ease this fabric into place.

Figure 24

When this part is taut and smooth, check the fabric around the outside of the wing rail, readjust if necessary by removing the tacks, then replace the tacks and drive them home. Make small cuts in the fabric where the top rail meets the back rail (see figure 24) so that the fabric can be pulled taut, folded and tacked neatly around it, and completely tucked between the webbing and the back rail. Leave the wings now until you have done the seat and back.

Figure 25

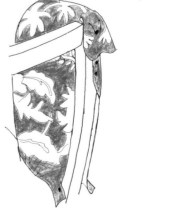

Figures 26–40 The seat

Figures 26 & 27 Attaching the webbing and springs

Some old chairs without seat cushions have very large springs in them — up to 350 mm (14 in). If this is the case, and your old springs are in good condition, you should use them again, since it is not always possible to buy such large ones. If you have to use shorter ones than this, attach the webbing to the top of the bottom rails instead of underneath them.

Now lay your springs in place on the webbing (in this case, in three rows of three with a slightly larger space left just behind the front rail). Make sure the knot in the top of each spring is positioned so that it will not rub against the hessian which will go over the springs. Anchor the springs to the webbing in the usual way.

Because of their size, these springs must be lashed at two levels. At the lower level lash the springs in both directions, anchoring the laid cord to the bottom rails and looping the cord around the waist of each spring at both sides. The springs should lean slightly toward the nearest rail, and the knots made exactly as described for the square armchair, project 6, figures 19 & 20. The second lashing should be through each spring in the usual way (**26**).

For the front rail springs we used four 175 mm (7 in) gauge 10 springs; you may need slightly smaller or larger ones but they should be slightly higher than the lashed seat springs when in position. Space these springs evenly across the front rail, and have them protruding slightly beyond the front edge of the rail. Anchor them to the rail (**27**) and lash them as described in project 6, figures 21–24.

Now cut a piece of cane as described in the introduction to project 6, or use the old one if it is still in good condition and attach it to the springs as described in project 6, figure 25.

Figure 28 Attaching the hessian

Following the instructions given in project 6, figures 26–34, you should now attach the hessian to the seat, using laid cord to anchor it between the main sprung section and the front edge springs. Note that, in this chair, the hessian is tacked to the outside of the back rail above the bottom one (i.e. the rail into which the top set of lashings are anchored) rather than the bottom rail as on the square armchair.

Figure 26

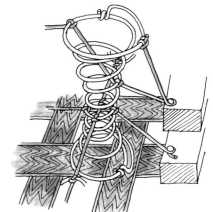

Figure 27

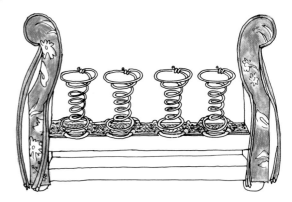

Pull the hessian down to the centre of the bottom front rail and put in temporary tacks about 75 mm (3 in) apart, making sure the hessian is smooth and straight (see figure 28). If necessary, trim the hessian here to about 50 mm (2 in) from the tacks. Pull the hessian through to the side rails, cutting and folding at the corners where necessary, and attach it with a row of temporary tacks to the top of the rail above the bottom one.

Using a springing needle and twine, attach the hessian to the cane and front springs with blanket stitches along the cane as shown in figure 28, then stitch all the seat springs to the hessian as described in project 4, figure 16, in the pattern shown in figure 28. Now thread a springing needle with a piece of laid cord 1·25 m (4 ft) long and sew each front spring to the nearest edge spring, pulling them together.

Figures 28–32 Putting on the padding

Stuff some ginger fibre down between the edge springs and the main springs until the fibre feels firm under the stitches you have just made (**28**). Remove the temporary tacks from the back rail of the seat, pull the hessian taut and drive in permanent tacks more closely spaced (say 13 mm (1 in) apart). Do the same along the side rails and trim the hessian. Tack around the back corners neatly. Remove the tacks from the bottom front rail, pull the hessian taut and retack permanently, adding more tacks as you go. Remove the tacks from the folded hessian at the sides of the front rail, pull it taut and tack it down. Make bridle ties over the seat and two more in a straight line across the front springs. Stuff handfuls of horsehair around these ties until you have a layer of hair 50 mm (2 in) thick (**29**).

Cut a piece of scrim about 150 mm (6 in) larger all round than the chair seat. Temporarily tack it to the same back rail as you did the hessian, pull it over the hair, tuck it in between the hair and the caned edge and anchor it with skewers. Pull the scrim down the sides of the chair, cutting and folding it around the front of the arms (see figure 30) and the back rails where necessary. Temporarily tack it to the top of the side rails above the bottom ones.

Thread a double bayonet needle with twine, push it into the seat about 100 mm (4 in) from one corner, pull it almost all the way out at the bottom, reangle it slightly and pull it out at the top, catching the padding and hessian together inside. Make two stitches like this along each side, then two in the centre (**30**).

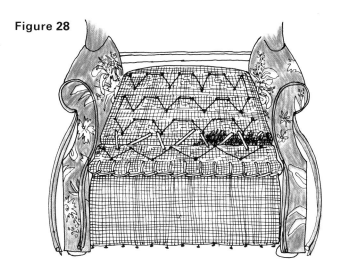

Figure 28

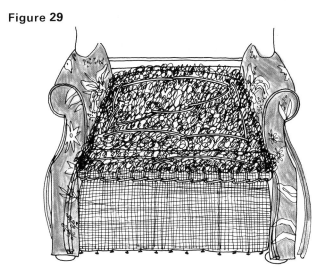

Figure 29

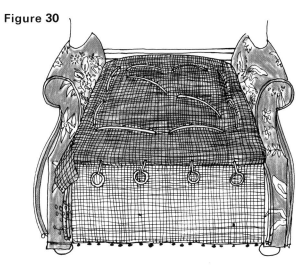

Figure 30

Project 7

Run a row of top stitches along the front edge of the seat, putting your needle into the edge right against the top surface of the cane and working as much hair forward as possible (**31**). Pull your stitches tight to give a firm edge roll about 50 mm (2 in) thick. Now drive home the temporary tacks holding the scrim to the side and back rails. Trim where necessary. With small pieces of horsehair, fill in the grooves in the top of the seat left by the top and anchoring stitches.

Cut a piece of skin wadding very slightly larger than the top of the seat, lay it in place and tuck it in; it does not need to be fastened down. Now do the same thing with a piece of linter felt, tearing and trimming it at the front edge to exactly the same size as the seat.

Cut a piece of Courtelle about 150 mm (6 in) larger all round than the top of the seat, place it in position and tuck it down at the sides and back, trimming and folding where necessary. It should tuck in so tightly that no anchoring is necessary. At the front, pull the Courtelle over the front of the chair and leave it (**32**).

Figures 33–40 Putting on the seat cover

Cut a piece of your covering fabric wide enough to go across the seat from rail to rail (the side rails where you tacked your hessian and scrim), and long enough to go from the tacking rail at the back to about 75 mm (3 in) below the top rail at the front.

Place the covering fabric in position, pull it through to the outside back and sides and temporarily tack it to the rails where the other layers have been anchored. Anchor it firmly in place with skewers along the front (**33**).

Now remove the temporary tacks from along one side of the seat, pull the front corner of fabric free and make a diagonal cut in it (**34**) so it will fit round the arm at the front. Push the fabric behind the cut back through to the outside. Repeat on the other side. Now remove the skewers at each side of the front edge and make a neat fold at both front corners, cutting into the fabric where necessary.

With a large springing needle and twine, and beginning at one end of the front section, sew down the fold you have made and stitch along the front edge, using running stitches and joining the covering fabric to the hessian on top of the cane. At the other end, sew down the corner fold in your final stitch as you did at the other corner (**35**).

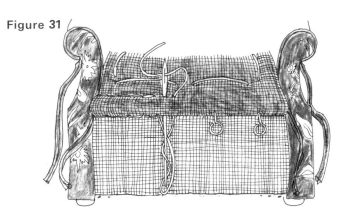

Figure 31

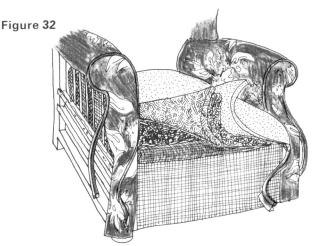

Figure 32

Figure 33

Figure 34

Measure and cut a piece of covering fabric the same width as the front panel, plus the arms, and long enough to go from your front edge stitching line to under the bottom rail. (Try to match the pattern, if there is one, to that on the seat.) Attach a strip of piping to the top edge of this piece and temporarily pin it in position on the front along the piped edge, anchoring it with skewers at the two front corners (**36**). Lift up this border and trim the seat fabric underneath it below the stitches, if necessary.

The front panel must now be padded. This padding really should be a layer of horsehair (fixed with bridle ties and covered with wadding and a layer of 115 g (4 oz) Courtelle (**37**)), but if you do not want to be bothered with this, simply tack a single layer of 230 g (8 oz) or a double layer of 115 g (4 oz) Courtelle over it.

Pull the covering fabric back down over the front panel and temporarily tack it along the bottom rail. Fold one end of the front panel back and make a diagonal cut in it as shown in figure 38, and another cut just below the piping (**38**) and pull the top two sections (piping and fabric) between the front of the seat and the arm. Pull the remainder of the fabric straight across the bottom of the arm under the front facing and temporarily tack it there (**39**). Repeat on the other side. If there are any hollows under this front panel, reach up and fill them in with linter felt or Courtelle. When you are satisfied with the look of this section, drive home the temporary tacks along the sides and bottom edges, adding more to make a really strong anchor.

Now release the temporary tacks holding the seat cover to the back rail, pull it taut and attach it with permanent tacks, stopping about 130 mm (5 in) short of the side rails. Pull the seat cover down through the side rails (**40**) and tack it permanently, again stopping 130 mm (5 in) short of the back rails.

Figure 35

Figure 36

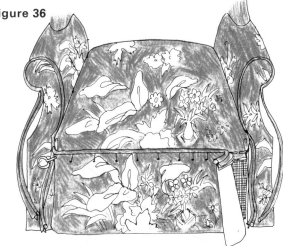

Figure 37

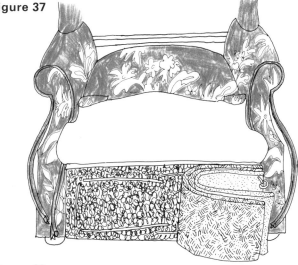

Figure 38

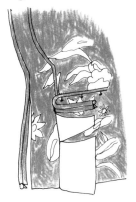

Figure 39

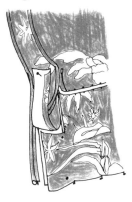

Figure 40

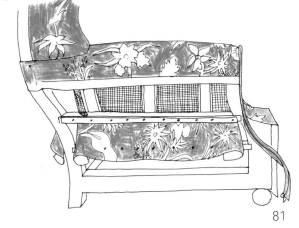

81

Project 7

At the two back corners of the seat, pull the covering fabric back through to the inside, carefully make diagonal cuts in from the corners so that the fabric can be folded round the back rails, pull the fabric to the outside again, round the back rails, then fold neatly and tack it to the rails permanently.

Slip-stitch the front panel to the seat cover along the piping and remove the pins and skewers holding it in place.

Figures 41–63 The back

Figures 41–43 Attaching the webbing and springs

Attach five parallel strips of webbing in the usual way from the top rail to the seat, starting with the strip in the middle. Now attach three rows horizontally. Your chair may require more or less webbing than this one; as a general rule, the strips should be approximately their own width apart (**41**). Leave out the turnings at the end of each strip, to avoid bulk under the final cover.

We have used nine 125 mm (5 in) gauge 12 springs; if the back is very much larger or smaller, the number you need may be different, but nine is the most usual for this type of chair. Put the springs in place on the webbing with the knots in the positions shown, and attach them in the usual way.

With doubled twine, lash the springs down the three rows vertically (**42**) and across the top two rows horizontally, as shown in figure 43. The arms of the chair will probably prevent you lashing the bottom horizontal row. If there is not enough room for the tacks to go in the usual position on top of the rails, put them into the sides as shown for the horizontal webbing (**43**) Note the angles at which the springs are lashed.

Figure 44 Attaching the hessian

Measure and cut a piece of hessian large enough to cover the back, over the springs (allowing for a hem), and attach it with permanent tacks or staples to the front face of the top and bottom rails. Remove temporary tacks where necessary, push the hessian down by the wings through to both sides (see figure 44) and temporarily tack it to the front face of the side rails, cutting and folding at the corners where necessary. With a springing needle and twine, attach the hessian to the springs in the usual way (**44**).

Figure 41

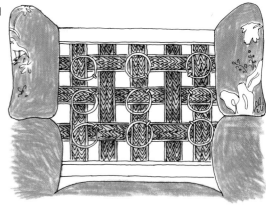

Figure 42

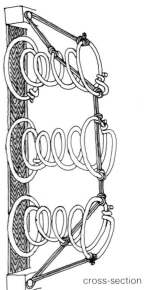

cross-section

Figure 43

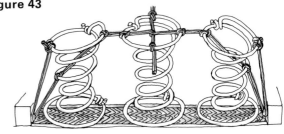

cross-section

Figure 44

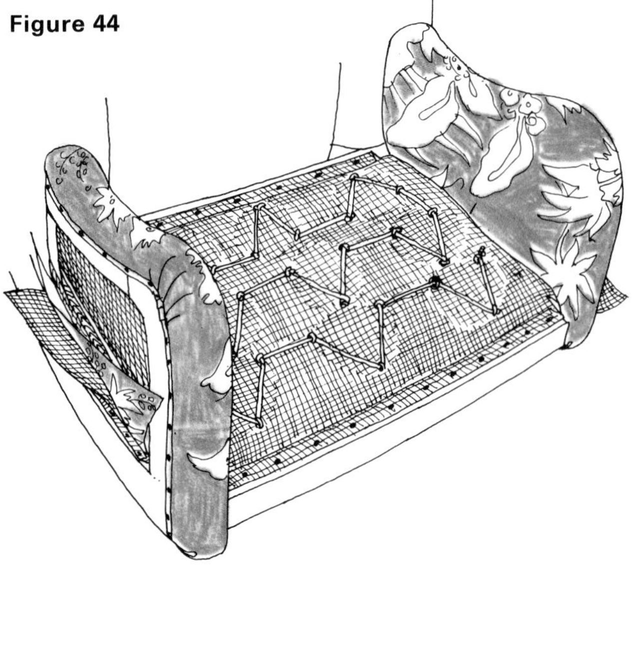

Figures 45–50 Putting on the padding

Now make bridle ties across the back, roughly following the random pattern laid out in the diagram (see figure 46).

Although it is usual to add stuffing now, then scrim, it is a good idea to anchor the scrim at the bottom of the back at this stage, since this is more difficult to do with the stuffing in place. Cut a piece of scrim about 150 mm (6 in) larger all round than the area of the back and tack it to the back face of the rail just above the seat, as shown in the cross-section (**45**). Fold it out of the way over the seat.

Now stuff handfuls of horsehair around the bridle ties in the usual way, until the distance from the padding on the back to the front edge of the seat measures 575 mm (23 in) when the scrim is pulled up over the back and fastened. (This gives the seat the right depth for comfort.) Using tacks and twine, make two bridle ties across the top rail of the back, loose enough to allow for a very thick layer of hair. Add horsehair around these ties (**46**) to make a firm, thick, soft layer along the top rail, blending into the hair over the back. When you are satisfied with the padding, pull the scrim over the hair and temporarily tack it in place along the outer face of the top rail near the bottom edge (**47**). Tuck the scrim a little way down the sides, by the wings.

With a double bayonet needle and twine, make large stitches across the back through all the layers, anchoring them together as you did with the seat (see figure 30), but in a zig-zag pattern. Take out the temporary tacks holding the scrim in place at the back, add more hair to the roll at the top if necessary, pull the scrim back over it firmly and temporarily tack again, this time along the outer edge of the top face of the top rail. Use your regulator needle to tease the hair into the roll and make it even and smooth. Work along the row of tacks from the middle out, releasing each one, adding more hair if necessary, turning the scrim neatly under and retacking permanently (**48**). At the corners, fold the scrim neatly, adding more hair if necessary, then tack it down. To reinforce this rolled edge, sew a row of top stitches along it in the usual way (**49** and **50**). Use your regulator often to pull the hair into the roll.

Tuck the scrim all the way down the sides, by the wings, cutting and folding it around the arm rails and back rails. Pull any loose hessian at the back to the nearest rail, tack it down and trim. Remove the tacks holding the scrim in place

Buttoned wing-chair

Figure 45

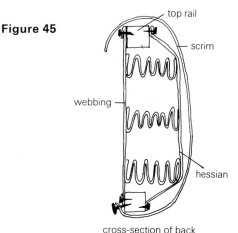

cross-section of back

Figure 46

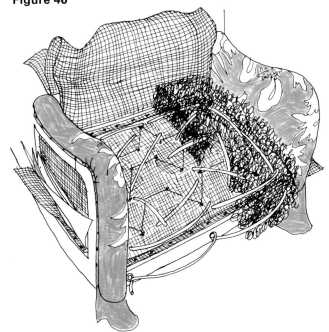

Figure 47 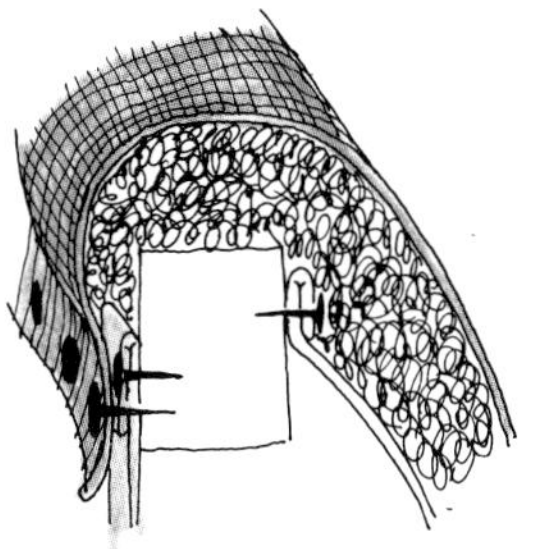 **Figure 48**

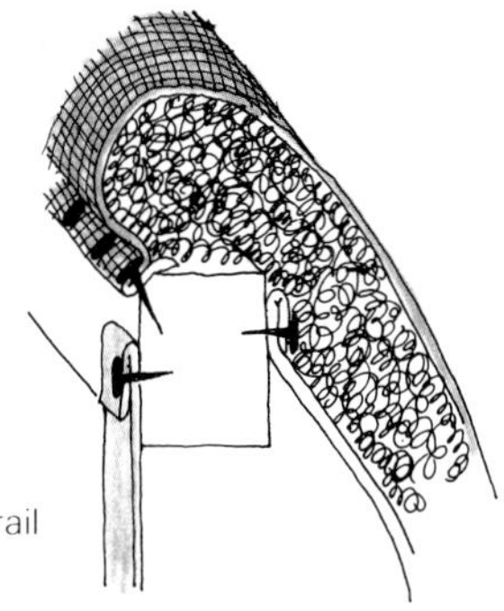

cross-sections of top back rail

Figure 49 **Figure 50**

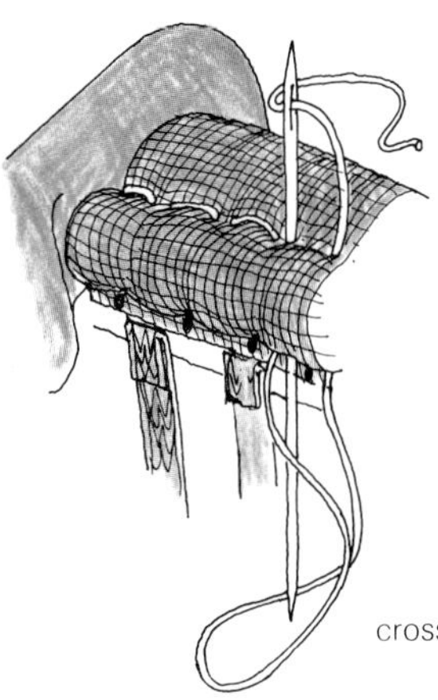

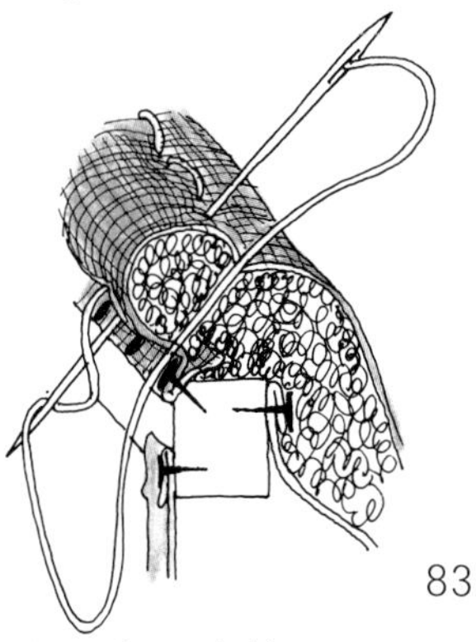

cross-sections of top stitching

83

Project 7

along the bottom, pull it taut and retack permanently. Pull the scrim through the wings, turn, and tack it along the same face as the hessian is tacked, cutting and folding where necessary.

Figures 51–63 Buttoning the back

Take the old back padding (or just the cover) which you have reserved and use it as a guide to mark the position of the buttons accurately on the scrim with a piece of chalk. Cut small holes in the scrim at each of these places with the point of a large pair of scissors.

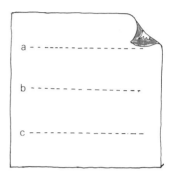

Figure 51

The buttons on our chair are 175 mm (7 in) apart. When marking their position on your covering fabric, you must allow for the amount of indentation made by the buttons and for the amount of give in your fabric. The maximum you should allow is 40 mm (1½ in) on either side of each button, and we have allowed this maximum because the padding will be quite thick and the fabric has a lot of give. (The minimum you should allow is 20 mm (¾ in).)

Figure 52

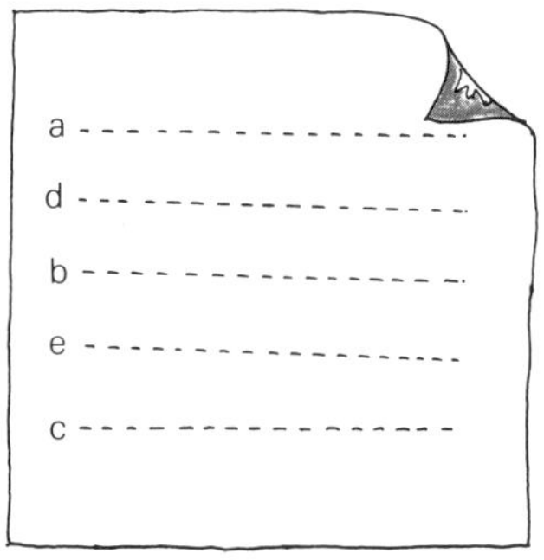

Measure the distance from the outer face of the top back rail, over the inside of the back, to the outer face of the rail above the bottom one, and from the outer face of one side rail, inside the wing, to the other side rail. Cut a piece of covering fabric 350 mm (14 in) longer and wider than this and lay it out flat, wrong side up, for marking.

Check the old cover to find the distance from the top of the fabric to the first row of buttons, and draw a horizontal line across the fabric this distance from the top (see figure 51). In our case, this is also 350 mm (14 in).

Figure 53

To arrive at the next marking, take the distance between the buttons (180 mm), add it to twice the appropriate allowance (2 x 40 mm = 80 mm) and draw a parallel line this distance (in this case 260 mm (10 in)) below the first one, and another the same distance again below this (**51**). These represent your main working lines which fall at alternate lines of buttoning. Now draw two more lines equally spaced between these as shown (**52**).

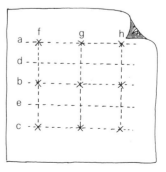

Figure 54

Mark the centre of the fabric crossways on the first three lines you drew (a, b and c) (**53**). Measure your working distance (distance between the buttons plus 2 x allowance (260 mm (10 in) in our case)) and mark this distance on either side of your centre points (**54**). Join these points diagonally as shown in figure 55 to give you the final positions of the buttons on the fabric. Mark these positions with pins (**55**) and tailor's tacks.

Figure 55

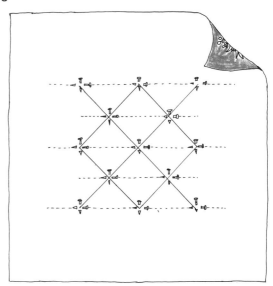

Cut a piece of 40 mm (1½ in) Supersoft foam slightly wider than the chair back and long enough to tuck behind the seat and go over the top to the outside face of the top rail. Place the foam in position and stick skewers in where the button-holes will go; do this by feeling under the foam for the holes you made in the scrim earlier. Make pencil or chalk marks where these holes should be (see figure 56), then remove the foam and cut the holes about the same size as your buttons (**56**). Tuck the foam back in place on the chair, press it over the top rail and tack it along the outside face. Measure and cut a piece of Courtelle about 150 mm (6 in) larger all round than the back of your chair and lay it in position. Feel through the Courtelle for the position of the holes and make holes in the Courtelle with your fingers.

Lay the back cover in place so that the tailor's tacks coincide with the holes. Beginning with the hole in the middle, attach the buttons in their positions, removing the tacks as you go. To do this, thread a 300 mm (12 in) double bayonet needle (or a straight buttoning needle) with twine and thread the button as shown in the diagram (**57**). Push the needle through the fabric, fold the fabric back, remove the tailor's tacks and push the needle through the hole and out at the back, making sure you go through a piece of webbing to make the button really secure. Anchor the twine round a tack driven into the nearest rail at the back, driven in lightly so the button can be adjusted later if necessary.

Figure 56

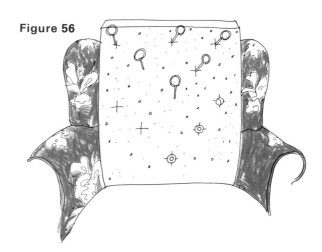

Figure 57

Anchor all the buttons in this way, pleating the fabric neatly between them on the inside and pinning the pleats in place as they are made (see figure 60). Do the top ones last.

When you have done all the buttoning, make sure all the buttons are at the same depth. If they are not, take out the temporary tacks holding the twine of any shallow ones, pull them tighter and retack. When they are all satisfactory, undo each tack and knot the two pieces of twine together on the webbing, tucking a small piece of hessian between the knot and the webbing to prevent the knot from

The Courtelle in position on the chair back.

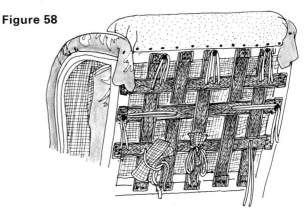

Figure 58

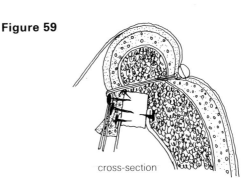

Figure 59

cross-section

Figure 60

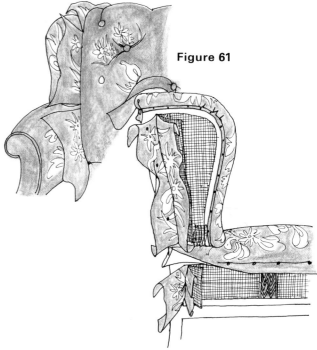

Figure 61

slipping through (**58**). Since the top three buttons on this chair come above the top rail, their twine goes through the foam, above the top rail, and will be anchored with tacks to the outside face of the top rail (**59**).

Pull the cover through to the outside at the bottom of the back. Now pull the cover over the top, arranging the pleats from the buttons neatly, and temporarily tack it to the outside face of the top back rail. Tuck the sides down slightly.

Make a cut into the fabric at the wing as shown, so it can be tucked through to the back above the arm rail (see figure 60). Now make a cut near the top, under the top wing rail, as shown (**60**), pull the fabric through between the wing and the back, and temporarily tack this piece to the side face of the side rail (figure 61). Pull the rest of the fabric through above the seat (**61**).

Make extra pleats from the outer top buttons to the nearest points on the wings and pin them in place. Cut, fold and trim the excess fabric at the top of the wing, tuck it in, and temporarily tack it to the outside face of the back rail, using your regulator for the tucking (**62**).

When you are satisfied with the fit of the back cover, add more tacks along the outer face of the top rail and drive all the tacks home, folding the fabric over neatly at the corners (**63**).

Figure 62

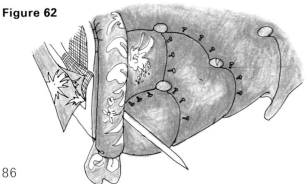

Figure 63

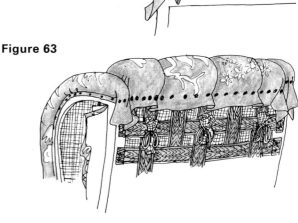

Pull the bottom of the back cover through to the outside face of the back rail above the bottom one, tack it in position and trim if necessary.

Figures 64-75 Finishing off

First, neaten the tops of the arms by checking any temporary tacks still in place, adjusting where necessary and tacking permanently.

Figure 64

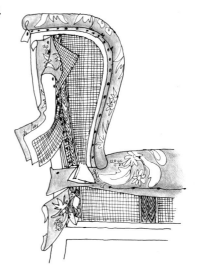

Figures 64-67 Finishing the wings

At the wings, remove the temporary tacks holding the back cover in place, pull the fabric taut and tack it permanently to the front face of the back rail. (All fastening down must be done to the front face of the rails to avoid bulk when the outer cover is on.) Trim if necessary (**64**). At the bottom of the wing, pull through the wing covering fabric and the hessian flap which has remained loose and attach them permanently to the arm rail. Tack down and trim any remaining ends of hessian or fabric still left (**65**).

Cut a piece of hessian large enough to cover the outside of the wing and tack it in position permanently.

Figure 65

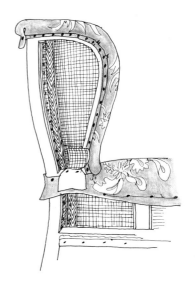

In order to attach the rest of the outside cover invisibly, it is necessary to use a method known as back-tacking. First, cut a rectangle of covering fabric about one and a half times larger than the area formed by the outside of the wing. Now cut a piece of back-tacking strip (or a narrow strip of card) long enough to go across the top of the wing. Place the fabric you have just cut in position on the outside of the wing and turn under a hem of about 25 mm (1 in) across the top. Keeping the hem in the same position (flat against the top wing rail), lift up the fabric from the bottom and tack this hem to the top of the rail just below the fold line. Put the back-tacking strip along this fold line and tack it in place to the rail. Now fold the fabric down over it, leaving a neat top edge. Pull the cover down to the bottom of the wing and anchor it with a temporary tack. Continue turning the fabric under and pressing it into place with your fingers around the curve — you will have to remove the tack, lift up the fabric and make a series of small cuts into the hem in order to do this neatly. Lift up the fabric again and attach a piece of Courtelle over the hessian (**66**). Pull the fabric back down, pin it in place round the curve, and fold and pin it down and round the back of the arm. Pull the fabric smoothly over the outside of

Figure 66

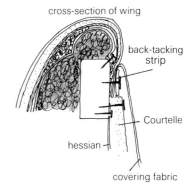

cross-section of wing

back-tacking strip

Courtelle

hessian

covering fabric

the wing and tack it permanently along the back face of the back rail (see figure 67).

Make a cut from the bottom outside corner up to the arm rail so you can pull the fabric down under the arm rail and anchor it permanently there. Slip-stitch all round the inside of the curve of the wing, down to the bottom of the roll at the top of the arm (**67**).

Figures 68–71 Finishing the arms

To finish off the arms, pull the piped front arm cover into place between the front panel and the arm, pin it there and slip-stitch the opening, taking in the piping. Pull the fabric tightly over the arm rail and permanently tack it to the outside face, taking in the piping which should be falling loose from the curve at the top of the arm. Fold and trim the fabric neatly at the bottom of the chair and tack it in place permanently (**68**).

For the outer arms, cut one piece of hessian and one of covering fabric about 50 mm (2 in) larger all round than the uncovered section. Now cut a strip of back-tacking the length of the arm rail. Place the fabric in position, turn under a hem at the top, fold back the fabric and tack it along the fold line, as you did at the top of the wing. Do exactly the same thing with the hessian, then, with a row of closely spaced tacks, permanently anchor your strip of back-tacking on top of these two layers to the underside of the top arm rail (**69**).

Pull the hessian down smoothly and tack it permanently to the surrounding rails, turning over a small hem, trimming and folding it at the corners where necessary (see figure 70).

Cut a piece of Courtelle about 25 mm (1 in) longer and the same width as the outer arm section. Turn over a 25 mm (1 in) hem at the top to cover the back-tacking strip. Tack it in position up the sides and along the bottom. If you have a staple gun, you may be able to put in a few staples along the top. There is no place here to put tacks, but the Courtelle should stay in place anyway (**70**). Trim the Courtelle to the shape of the outside arm section.

Pull the covering fabric down firmly and temporarily tack it under the bottom rail (see figure 71). Now pull it towards the back and temporarily tack it to the back face of the back rail. Pull the fabric towards the front and fasten it with a temporary tack underneath the front rail. Pull the rest of the fabric forward so that it is taut and pin it in position temporarily, with the

Figure 67

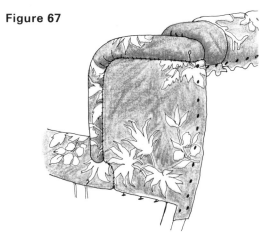

Figure 68

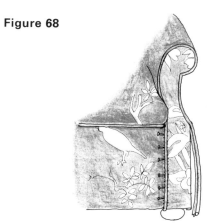

Figure 69

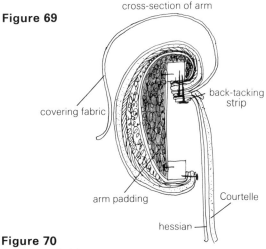

cross-section of arm

back-tacking strip

covering fabric

arm padding

Courtelle

hessian

Figure 70

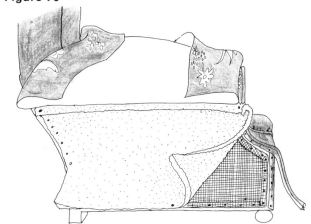

raw edges out (see figure 71). Trim any excess fabric, cut into the curves, then remove each pin, beginning from the top. Turn under a hem and repin.

When you are satisfied with the look of the outside arm, drive the tacks home at the bottom and the back, adding more as you go so your fixing will be secure. Slip-stitch the front edge of this panel in place where you have pinned it (**71**).

Figure 71

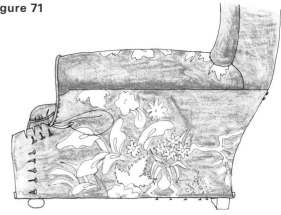

Figures 72–75 Finishing off the back and the base

Attach the final cover to the back with the hessian and the tacking strip in the same way as you did with the outside arm panels, but this time attach the layers to the outside face of the rail. To fit round the curve formed by the padding, cut into the strip as shown in the diagram (**72**). The sharper the curve, the smaller and more acute these cuts should be.

Figure 72

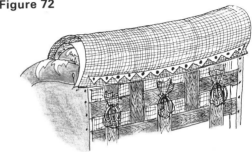

Tack the hessian down all around, turning over a small hem, then add a layer of Courtelle, turning over a small hem at the top as before and tacking all around — this time you will be able to anchor it along the top as well (**73**).

Figure 74

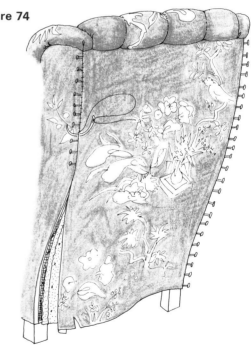

Figure 73

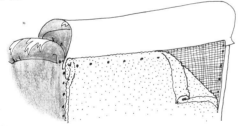

Pull the covering fabric down over the Courtelle, pull it taut at the sides, pin, trim, then turn under hems and re-pin as before. Slip-stitch this back panel to the sides (**74**).

Turn the chair upside-down and, beginning in the middle of each rail, tack down the covering fabric permanently to the four bottom rails, adding extra tacks for strength. Cut and fold the fabric neatly around the legs and trim any excess.

Measure and cut a piece of black upholsterer's linen or hessian slightly larger than the bottom of your chair. Turning under a small hem, tack this in position, cutting and folding it round the legs where necessary (**75**).

Figure 75

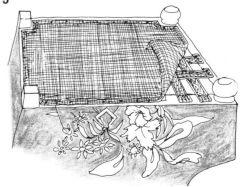

Project 8
Chesterfield

Introduction

Before you begin this project, read the introduction to project 6 for a general outline of the steps. The techniques are also very similar to some of those for project 7.

Tools

scissors
pencil
tape-measure
hammer
webbing stretcher
springing needle
skewers
double bayonet needle
pins
slipping needle
tailor's chalk
paper (for template of arm fronts)
rasp
regulator needle

Materials

black and white first-quality webbing: see
 project 2, figure 3 for measurements and add
 500 mm (20 in)
20 mm ($\frac{5}{8}$ in) tacks
10 mm ($\frac{3}{8}$ in) and 13 mm ($\frac{1}{2}$ in) fine tacks
springs: we used twenty-four 225 mm (9 in)
 gauge 8 ones for the seat, thirteen 150 mm
 (6 in) gauge 10 upright and twelve 175 mm
 (7 in) leaning springs for the top of the arms
 and back, and twelve 150 mm (6 in) gauge 12
 ones for the inner arms and back
twine
laid cord
galvanized staples
hessian — enough to cover the sprung areas of
 the arms, back and seat (see figures 11 and
 31–33)

90

ginger fibre for padding the back and round the seat springs — use the old stuffing to estimate quantities

scrim — enough to cover the padded arms, back and seat (see figures 19 and 31)

covering fabric — enough to go over all surfaces of the padded sofa and attach to the frame (see figures 21–23 and 31–35)

curtain heading tape (see figure 23)

linter felt — small pieces to fill in hollows and large pieces to cover the whole sprung section of arms and back, and the seat

sheet (skin) wadding — enough to cover the sprung arms and back, the seat and the front panel

60 g (2 oz) Courtelle — enough to cover the sprung arms and back, the seat, the front panel, and facings

horsehair for the seat and front panel — use the old stuffing to gauge approximately how much you need

piping cord — enough to extend along the front border of the seat plus 300 mm (12 in), and round the facings

6 mm ($\frac{1}{4}$ in) thick plywood, for the front facings

contact adhesive

30 mm ($1\frac{1}{4}$ in) panel pins

back-tacking strip or strip of card, long enough to go along the outer back and wings, along the top rails

Project 8

Figures 1 & 2 Attaching the seat springs

Although it is the usual practice to do the arms of a piece of upholstered furniture first, in this case you should attach the webbing and seat springs first, before going on to the arms and back. This is because, if the thick padding were put on the arms and back first, it would prevent you reaching the bottom rails on to which the seat springs are lashed.

See figure 1 for the parts of the frame referred to throughout this project. Having stripped the frame bare (**1**), attach webbing to the bottom rail across the seat area, as described in project 2, figures 3–8, remembering to place the strips their own width apart. If there are strips of wood across the frame, position the webbing over them and place the springs on the webbing as shown (**2**); otherwise, position them in the usual way, at the junctions of the webbing. Leave room at the sides and back for the arm and back padding. Stitch the springs to the webbing and lash them together firmly, as described in project 4, steps 2–12.

Figures 3–30 Upholstering the arms and back

The skills involved in springing the arms and making the roll along the top of the arms and back are introduced here.

Figures 3 & 4 The top rail springing

Springs must first be positioned along the top rail in order to support the padding which will go along the top of the arms and back. These springs are attached in a similar way to those on the front edge of a sprung armchair, but with alternate springs leaning in towards the centre of the sofa at a 45° angle, to provide support for the inside top edge.

First place the upright springs in position: start by putting one at the front of each arm and one at each corner. Now add more upright ones, leaving room for an angled spring between each one. There will not be enough room at the corners for an angled spring to bend inwards on both sides, so put an upright spring at each end of the back rail (so that there are two uprights next to each other at the back corners). If the base of the springs is wider than the back rail, they should protrude towards the centre of the sofa rather than to the outside. Now anchor each spring to the rail all round with at least three galvanized staples (see figure 4).

Figure 1

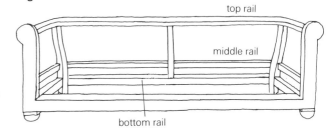

top rail

middle rail

bottom rail

Figure 2

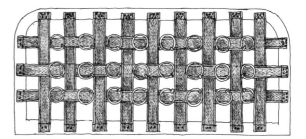

Place one angled spring between each upright one and tack it to the rail with galvanized staples in the same way. If you are not using the old springs (which will already be the right shape), you should bend each one at the waist to the correct angle before placing it on the rail. After putting each one on the rail, hammer the bottom coil over the inside of the rail (**3**). Place a length of webbing along the top rail and tack it down round the base of the springs (**4**), as described for the front rail springs in project 6, figures 21–24.

Figure 3

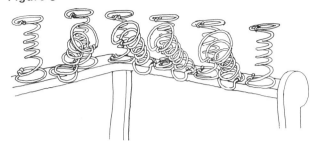

Figure 5 Webbing the back and arms

Attach a piece of webbing horizontally halfway between the top and the middle rail, both across the back of the chesterfield and across each arm. Now attach strips of webbing vertically, one directly under each angled spring, anchoring the webbing round the middle rail and pulling it up over the bottom coil of each angled spring. Anchor these rows of vertical webbing to the outside face of the top rail (**5**).

Figure 4

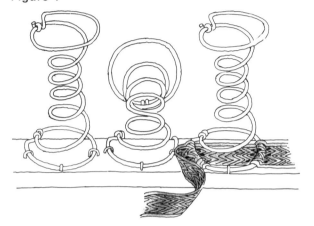

Figure 6 Attaching the back and arm springs

Using the method described in project 4, figures 2–5, anchor springs to the webbing you have just attached, one at each point where the vertical strips cross the horizontal ones (**6**). (We used three for each arm and six across the back.)

Figure 5

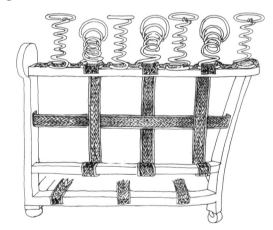

Figures 7 & 8 Lashing the upright top rail springs

Again referring to the instructions for front rail springs (project 6, figures 21–24), first lash only the upright springs to the rail, running the cord outside the angled springs between tacks as shown in figure 7.

Cut another length of laid cord (with a piece of furniture this large it would be awkward to work with a piece of cord long enough to do the job in one go, so the precise length is not important) and anchor it round a tack at the top of one arm at the front in the usual way, knotting the short end to the top of the front spring as shown (figure 7). Loop the cord round the waist of the first upright spring at the nearest point. Then, using simple knots, knot it to the top coil at the furthest point and continue knotting it to opposite sides of the top coil of each upright spring. At the corners, knot the twine round the top coil at the nearest point, then loop it round

Figure 6

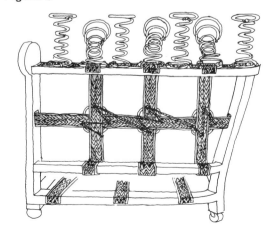

the waist. Take it down to the rail, anchor it with
a tack, then loop it round the waist of the next
upright (**7**). Continue along the back and
second arm in exactly the same way.

Now, with a piece of cord, tie each corner spring
to the first back spring as shown (**8**), as they
have not yet been lashed together at the top.

Figure 9 Lashing the angled top rail springs

To lash each angled spring at the top rail to the
back and arm springs directly below it, cut a
length of twine about 2 m (78 in) long and
double it. Drive a temporary tack into the inner
face of the middle rail directly below these
springs, as shown in figure 9. Loop your doubled
twine round the waist of the lowest spring,
twist it round the temporary tack and drive it
home, then knot it round the top coil of the same
spring, first on one side, then on the other as
shown in figure 9. Take the twine up to the
angled spring above, knot it round the top coil at
the nearest point, then opposite. Pull the twine
taut and anchor it to the outside edge of the top
face of the top rail (**9**).

Figure 10 Lashing the back and arm springs

The springs on the inside back and arms should
now be lashed horizontally. Cut a single piece of
twine one and a half times the length of the
back and arms. Anchor the end of it with a tack
to the inner face of one of the arm fronts in line
with these springs. Leave enough twine loose so
that you can knot it to the top coil of the nearest
spring when you have finished the lashing. Loop
the twine at the waist of the first spring, then
knot it to the top coil at the furthest point, then
to the top of the next spring at the nearest point.
Now loop it round the lashing which runs
vertically, then knot it to the top coil on the
opposite side (**10**). Continue in this way along
the back and arms and finish by anchoring the
twine to the other arm front, leaving enough
twine to tie back to the top coil firmly. Tie the
other end you left at the beginning to the top of
the first spring, as shown in figure 10.
Now lash the angled springs along the top rail
to each other in the same way (see figure 10).

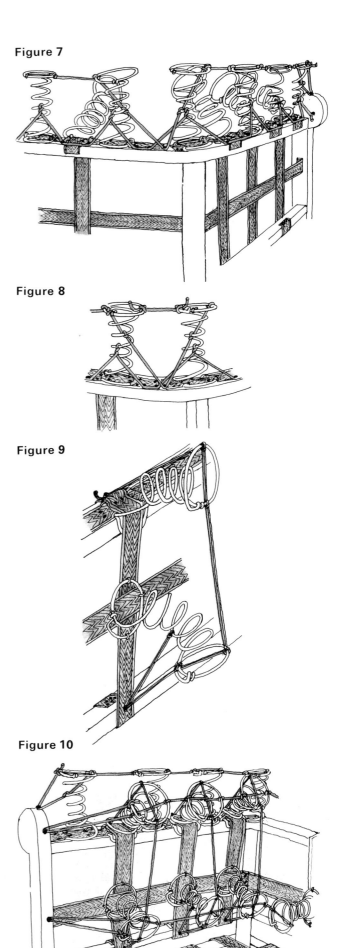

Figure 7

Figure 8

Figure 9

Figure 10

Figures 11–16 Attaching hessian to the arms and back

Cut two pieces of hessian slightly wider than the arms of the chesterfield and long enough to go from the outer face of the middle rail, under the rail, up over the inside arm to the outer face of the top rail. Turning over a hem, temporarily tack the hessian at one arm to the outer face of the middle rail. Pull it under this rail, up over the springs – see the cross-section (**11**) – and temporarily tack it to the outer face of the top rail. Pull the hessian forward firmly and temporarily tack it to the inner face of the front arm (figure 12). Cut and fold the hessian round the middle rail where necessary. At the inner corners, cut into the hessian at top and bottom where the two pieces of horizontal lashing fall (**12**), so that it can be tucked through to the back rail.

Cut a piece of hessian to cover the back in the same way, and lay it in position. Attach it to the rails in the same way as before (figure 11), except that you will have to cut it at the bottom of the central vertical rail at the back, to attach it to the middle rail. At the inner corners place the hessian over the side pieces and make two cuts as shown (**13**). Pull the three resulting sections

Figure 11

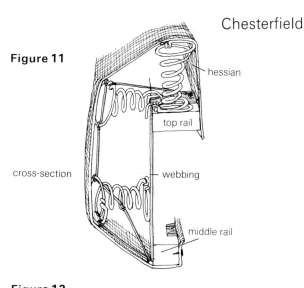

Figure 12

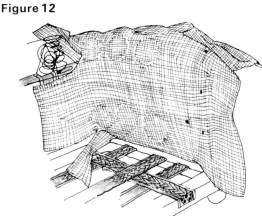

Figure 13

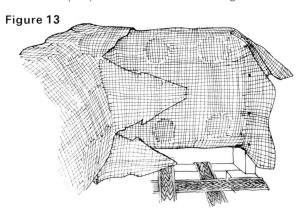

Figure 14

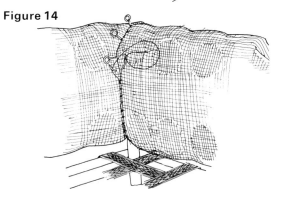

through to the back of the sofa, one above the top rail, one between the top and middle rail, and one below the middle rail. Tack them down out of the way, trimming any excess hessian at the corners but leaving enough to fold the back and arm sections neatly together along the inner corner, over the top and down the back. Anchor this fold with skewers as shown in figure 14, and, starting from the inside bottom, stitch along this fold (**14**), up the inner corner, over the top and down the outside to the level of the top rail (**15**).

Figure 15

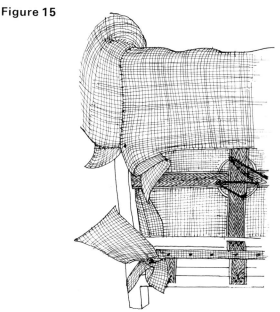

95

Project 8

Trim the hessian to just above the temporary tacks along the middle rail, then remove the tacks, pull the hessian taut, turn over a small hem and replace the tacks, driving them home. Add more between the existing ones so that the hessian is attached firmly all round the sofa to the outer face of the middle rail.

Now trim the hessian to just beyond the front of the arm and the side of the top rail, turn over a small hem and tack it firmly in place with permanent tacks all round the arm, so that the front face is fully exposed (**16**).

Using a springing needle and twine, anchor the springs to the hessian as described in project 4, figure 18.

Figure 16

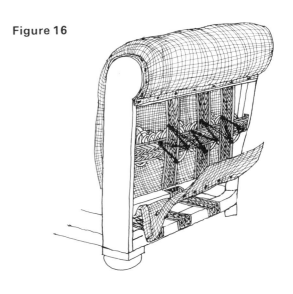

Figures 17 & 18 The first layer of padding

To provide an anchor for the padding, cover the hessian with bridle ties in the pattern shown (**17**).

Take handfuls of ginger fibre and tuck them under and around the bridle ties you have just made (**18**) until the entire area of hessian is covered and each section of fibre is blended well into the next. At this stage, the fibre should be about 100 mm (4 in) thick and feel very firm and solid. There is no special technique for dealing with the corners; just continue stuffing the fibre around the ties without a break, following the line of the chesterfield.

Figure 17

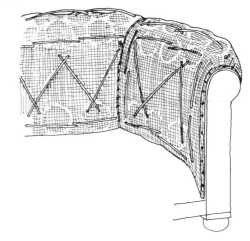

Figures 19 & 20 Attaching the scrim

Cut three pieces of scrim (one for each arm and one for the back) 100 mm (4 in) larger all round than the area (rail to rail, over the padding) to be covered. Anchor them in position with temporary tacks in exactly the same way as you anchored the hessian (see figure 11). Adjust the scrim to fit neatly, removing the temporary tacks where necessary and cutting into the scrim exactly as you did with the hessian, pulling it into position until it is smooth and taut over the fibre. If there are any lumps or hollows, add more fibre or redistribute the existing fibre with the point of a regulator.

To reinforce the edges of the padded area, you must make a row of blind stitches, then a row of top stitches, round the front face of the arms (see figures 19 and 20). Full instructions for these stitches are given in project 3, figures 18–28. Now anchor the padding to the hessian along the inside back and arms with large running stitches, as shown in project 7, figure 8.

Figure 18

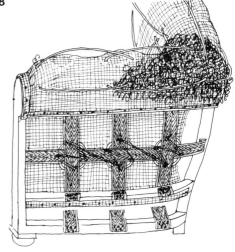

Fold the scrim at the corners and stitch (**19**) as you did with the hessian (see figure 15).

To reinforce the roll formed by the top of the arms and back, make a row of blind stitches all along the roll in the position shown (**20**).

Remove the temporary tacks holding the scrim in place and adjust if necessary. Replace the tacks and drive them home, adding more where necessary to make a firm edge.

Figures 21-23 Making up the cover

To make the arm covers, measure and cut two pieces of covering fabric 150 mm (6 in) longer than the scrim which covers the same area. To find the necessary width, measure along the outside arm from the front to the outside back corner of the roll, at the back rail, and add 75 mm (3 in).

For the back cover, measure the length in the same way as for the arms (i.e. scrim plus 150 mm) and the width from the seam on the scrim at one back corner to the other, plus 150 mm (6 in). If the fabric is not wide enough to cover this area, have one large panel in the middle and two smaller ones at each side, matching the pattern, if any.

Fold the back piece of fabric in half and make a small nick in the middle of the top edge. Lay the back piece in position, right side up, centring the seams and matching the nick to the central rail. Temporarily tack it in place to this central rail.

To establish the point where the seams should fall, attach a piece of twine with a tack driven into each vertical back rail just below the middle horizontal one. Bring the twine up to the inside, over the padding to the back, and anchor it to the back rail just below the scrim (**21**).

Lay the back piece of fabric over the twine at each corner and trim any excess to about 40 mm (1½ in) beyond the twine, but trim it only as far as the top of the seat, since you will need this excess fabric to tuck down the sides and back. With skewers, anchor this back piece in position along the line of twine. Now lay the arm pieces in position and temporarily tack them to the bottom face of the top rail. Anchor them with skewers to the padding at the front of the arm, as shown in figure 22, then trim the excess fabric at the corners to about 40 mm (1½ in) beyond the twine, down to the top of the seat.

At the inner corners pin the arm and back pieces together to make a neat fit, with seam allowances

Figure 19

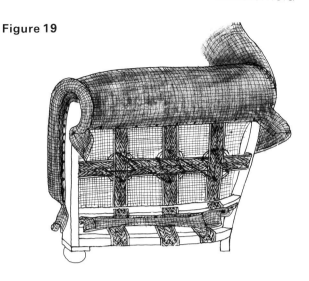

Figure 20

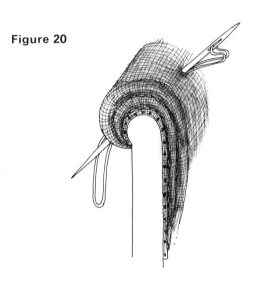

Figure 21

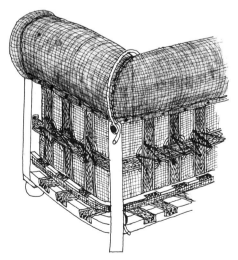

facing out. Trim the seam allowances to 13 mm ($\frac{1}{2}$ in), again to the top of the seat, and make small nicks in the seam allowances every 100 mm (4 in) so that you can match the fabric when you take it off and put it right sides together for sewing (**22**). Carefully remove the cover, turn the pieces right sides together and re-pin, matching nicks. Now stitch the seams, catching in each one a length of curtain heading tape extending about 250 mm (10 in) beyond each end of the seam (**23**). This will help you pull the cover neatly into position at the corners.

Figures 24–26 The final padding

Tear off small pieces of linter felt and lay them in the grooves formed by the top stitching at the front of the arms and in the hollows made by the anchoring stitches on the back and sides (see figure 24). Now tear off enough linter felt in large sheets to cover the inner arms and back, and go right over the curve to the top rail, but not over the front edge of the arm (**24**). When you join pieces, butt them together; do not overlap them. There is no need to fasten the linter felt down.

Cut three pieces of skin wadding, one to go over each arm and one to go over the back. Lay them in position and anchor the arm pieces to the side face of the top rail with a few tacks, and tuck it down behind the seat. At the front of the arms, pull it over the front and gather it where necessary round the curve, attaching it with a few tacks (see figure 25). Overlap the pieces of wadding to join them and cut into them where necessary at the inner corners. Cover the wadding with a layer of Courtelle attached in exactly the same way (**25**). The cross-section (**26**) shows where all the layers are attached.

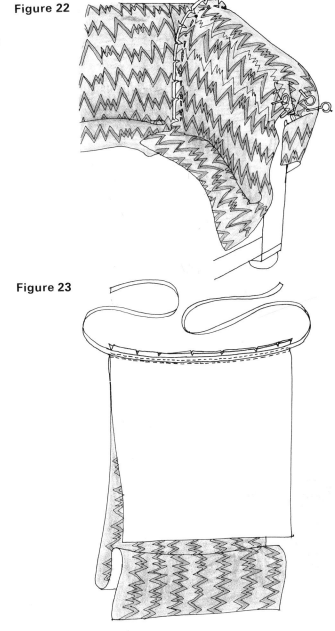

Figure 22

Figure 23

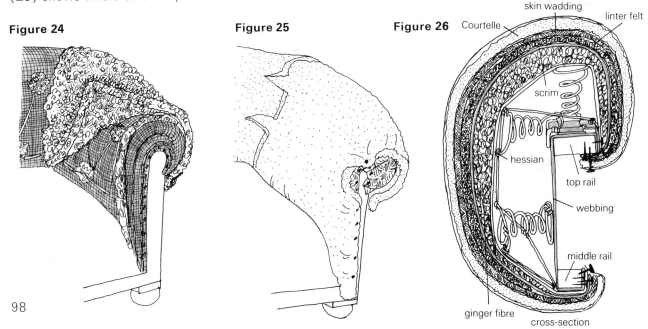

Figure 24

Figure 25

Figure 26

skin wadding

linter felt

Courtelle

scrim

hessian

top rail

webbing

middle rail

ginger fibre

cross-section

Figures 27–30 Attaching the cover

Put the made-up cover in place on the chesterfield. Pull it down taut at the outer corners with the tapes and put a temporary tack through each top tape into the outside face of the back rail to keep it there. Pull the cover into position at the front of the arms and anchor it with a temporary tack to the outer and front faces of the front rail. Push the bottom tape down into the inside corners, pull it through to the outside corner of the arms and temporarily tack it to the outer face of the back rail (**27**).

Pull the cover over the top of the sofa to the back and, starting at the centre, drive a row of temporary tacks into the bottom face of the top rail all round, making neat and symmetrical pleats at both back corners (**28**). Smooth the cover round the inside back and arms and tuck it down behind the seat. At the centre of the back, cut in from the bottom so that the cover can be pulled round the upright rail (figure 29).

Pull the fabric through to the outside back, pull it taut and fasten it with temporary tacks to the outside face of the middle back rail (**29**).

At the front of each arm, pull the fabric firmly towards the centre, making even, neat pleats in the same direction (use your regulator to help) and temporarily tack them in place. These tacks should be placed about 6 mm ($\frac{1}{4}$ in) from the edge of the padding so that they go directly into the wood. When you are working on the second arm, measure from the floor to the first inside pleat to make sure that it is on the same level as the one on the first arm. When you are satisfied that the pleats are even and straight, drive the tacks home and add more to make a close row all the way round them (**30**). Trim the fabric.

At the bottom front of the inside arm, make two cuts up from the bottom of the fabric as shown in figure 30 so you can pull the fabric down round the front rail to the outside. It is a good idea to begin by making a short cut, then lengthen it bit by bit. Cut, fold and neaten.

Figures 31–35 Upholstering the seat, front panel and facings

The seat

To attach the padding and covering to the seat follow the instructions for project 7, figures 26–40. The only difference here is that if one width of fabric will not cover the chesterfield seat, you will have to add two small panels at each side as you did with the back.

Figure 27

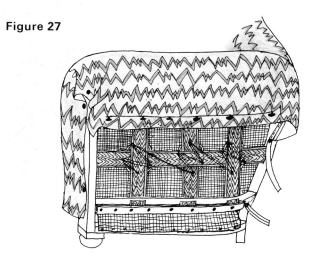

Figure 28

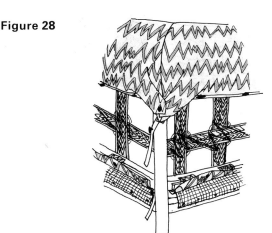

Figure 29

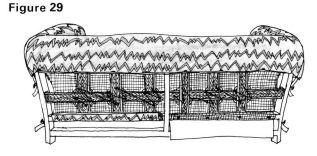

Figure 30

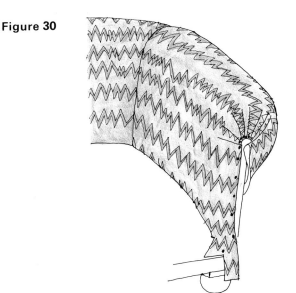

Figures 31–33 The front panel

Cut a piece of covering fabric large enough to go from under the front edge roll of the seat to the bottom of the front rail, plus 50 mm (2 in), and right across the front of the chesterfield. If your fabric is not wide enough, you will have to sew a narrow piece on either side of a central piece as you did with the back and the seat. Attach a length of piping along the top edge of this panel, extending about 150 mm (6 in) on either side. (See project 1, figures 21–25.)

Figure 31

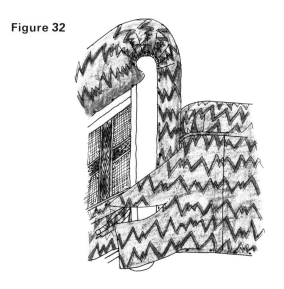

Lay the fabric panel in place across the front of the chesterfield and anchor it with skewers (matching any seam lines with those on the seat). Fold the fabric back over the seat. Using your springing needle and twine, make bridle ties across the hessian (attached to the front panel when you padded the seat), and stuff them with a fairly thin layer of horsehair in the usual way (figure 31). Cover this with a piece of skin wadding large enough to lay over the top, tuck down at each side between the seat and the arms, and fasten over the bottom rail. Anchor this at the top with skewers, tuck it down the sides and tack it to the front of the bottom rail. Now add a layer of 60 g (2 oz) Courtelle, cut to the same size. Anchor it under the same skewers that go through the wadding, tuck it down the sides and tack it along the bottom (**31**).

Figure 32

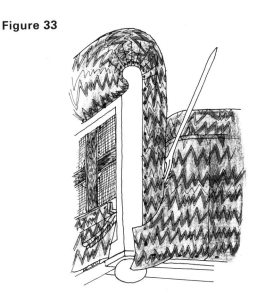

Remove the skewers. This top line of the padding remains unattached. Fold the covering fabric for the border down into place and anchor the piped edge under the front roll with large pins or skewers stuck straight in. Pull the border down gently and temporarily tack it to the bottom face of the bottom front rail.

Cut in from each side of the border just below the piping to about 75 mm (3 in) before you get to the seat. Push this piping down between the seat and the arm and pull it to the outside (as shown in figure 32) by reaching up underneath the middle rail at the outside arm.

Figure 33

Cut into the front panel from the side to a point near the top of the bottom rail (**32**). Fold the fabric under to make a continuous curve coming down from the top corner of the seat. You may need to push a little stuffing in here to make a smooth curve. When you are satisfied that the front border is smooth and straight, slip-stitch it to the seat along the piping, using the blunt end of your regulator to push the fabric between the arm and the front border (**33**), then tack it permanently below the bottom rail. At the bottom corners, trim and fold the fabric at the inside leg (see figure 34).

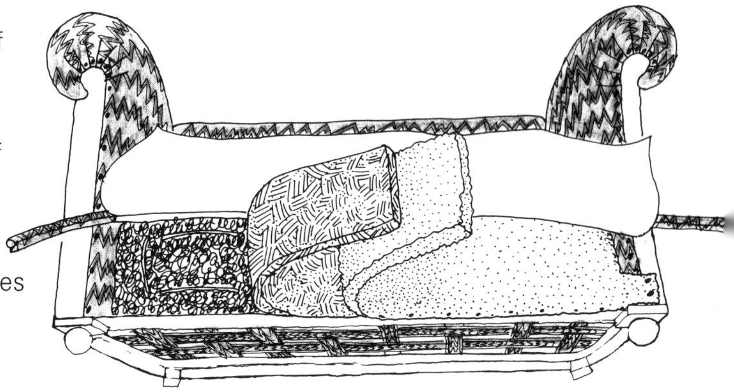

Figures 34 & 35 Making the front facings

Cut a paper template to the scroll shape formed by the front faces of the arms, about 13 mm ($\frac{1}{2}$ in) beyond the row of tacks and extending to the bottom of the front of the arm, flush with the outside edge, as shown (**34**). Tack it lightly to two pieces of 6 mm ($\frac{1}{4}$ in) plywood in turn, trace round them carefully and cut out the shapes with a jigsaw or hacksaw. These two pieces of plywood become the facings.

Chamfer the front edges of the facings all round with a rasp, so there will be no noticeable edge when it is covered with fabric. Cut a piece of Courtelle the same size as each facing and glue it to the front. Place each facing, padded side down, on a piece of covering fabric, wrong side up. Cut the fabric about 50 mm (2 in) beyond the facing, wrap it round the facing except at the straight inner edge and fasten it with staples: you will have to make a cut underneath the curve so that the fabric will stretch smoothly (see figure 35). When the fabric is stapled down, trim it close to the staples, leaving the loose flap.

Make up some piping long enough to go all round the facings. Unpick the piping about 25 mm (1 in) at one end and cut off the end of the cord inside. Fold the fabric down over the top of the cord and then in half lengthways to neaten. Lay this along the straight side of the facing, at the back (**35**) and fasten it down with 10 mm ($\frac{3}{8}$ in) fine tacks or staples. Take the piping round the facing, cutting into the curves.

Attaching the facings to the arms

Place the facing in position on the arm, lift up the loose flap and attach the facing under the fabric with 13 mm ($\frac{1}{2}$ in) fine tacks placed as far in as you can reach from the edge. The heads of the tacks will be hidden under the fabric. Now anchor the facing to the inside front of the arm by driving 30 mm ($1\frac{1}{4}$ in) panel pins through the fabric into the wood. It is very important that these pins remain straight so they can be concealed. When you have driven them in, use the point of a pin to ease the fabric free of the head of the pin, so that it is no longer visible.

Pull the loose flap of fabric round to the outside arm and tack it in place along its length. Pull the loose piping down and fasten it in place along the outside edge where you tacked the fabric. Trim and neaten the piping.

The outer arm and back covers are back-tacked and slip-stitched, and the project finished off, in exactly the same way as project 7.

Figure 34

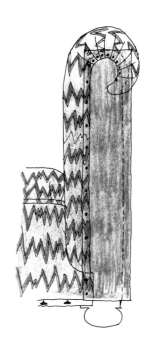

Figure 35

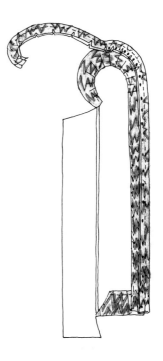

Care, repairs and finishing

Upholstery fabrics

The time and care you put into your upholstery work will be wasted if you choose a covering fabric which is not strong enough for furniture. Many pretty materials are really only suitable for curtaining, and even those which can be made into loose covers are often too thin or loosely woven for tight upholstery, so be sure to check with your supplier before you buy.

There is a huge range of fibres to choose from and each has its own peculiarities; fibre content must, by law, be marked on all fabric, so you should have no difficulty in finding one to meet your needs.

Natural fabrics

These fabrics are made from fibres that come either from plants, like cotton and linen, or from animals, like wool and silk. They have many

Make sure that any pure cotton you choose for upholstery is strong and tightly woven.

Top: for a crisp look use linen as a covering fabric and add contrast piping. Above, left: wool is expensive but wears well and resists burning. Above, right: linen union in a traditional print is appropriate for a chesterfield.

advantages but are in some cases becoming scarcer and more expensive, and you will find that many suitable materials are now made from a combination of natural and artificial fibres.

Wool Used extensively for upholstery, wool has many advantages as a furnishing fabric. Because it lacks the static electricity of many artificial fibres, it attracts less dirt. It is very tough and has a natural resilience which helps it to keep its appearance even after several years of hard wear.

This fabric is used widely for contract jobs such as hotels and airports, not only because it is soft and warm to sit on, but also because it has a natural and very efficient flame resistance: a lighted cigarette dropped on to wool will

smoulder and die, rather than flare up as it would with many synthetics. Wool absorbs moisture easily and therefore takes dyes readily, so it can be made in an enormous range of colours and patterns.

Almost all furnishing wool sold by the metre will have been treated with a moth-proofing solution; but make sure that this is so. All materials which show the Woolmark (pure new wool) or Woolblend mark (at least 70 per cent pure new wool) will have had this treatment; these are trade marks of the International Wool Secretariat.

Wool should be dry-cleaned and any spots treated with a slightly dampened cloth, since over-wet wool tends to become lumpy and matted.

Cotton An easy material to care for, pure cotton has to be extremely thick, strong and closely woven to be suitable for tight covering. Stiff, glazed cotton, called chintz, used to be popular for upholstery, but it has become very expensive in recent years. The glaze will eventually come off if you clean it with water and you may have difficulty finding a company willing to reglaze the fabric.

Linen A vegetable product like cotton, linen is rather more expensive and somewhat coarser; it also loses it strength more quickly than cotton when wet, and creases if not specially treated. Not all linen is suitable for upholstery.

Linen Union This material has a cotton warp and a linen weft. (Warp threads run along the length of a fabric, while weft threads run across its length.) When two different fibres are woven together in this way, the fabric is described as a 'mix' (as opposed to a 'blend', where each thread is comprised of two or more different fibres). Linen union is a very common and highly suitable fabric for upholstery and comes in a huge range of traditional and modern prints and plain colours.

Silk Too weak to be used as a tight covering on its own, silk is often mixed with tougher fibres such as linen and cotton for upholstery fabrics.

Velvet Although widely used in the last century as an upholstery fabric, real velvet (as opposed to its synthetic imitators) is not really suitable for people who give their furniture a great deal of hard wear, since under these conditions the pile is quite likely to be rubbed off. Velvet also has a tendency to show 'shading' — patches of apparently lighter or darker fabric caused by a change of the direction in which the pile runs.

Artificial fabrics

Science has brought us many new, chemically produced materials which relieve the huge demand for natural fabrics and often help to give these fabrics properties which they would not have on their own. Artificial fibres can be divided into two main groups, regenerated and synthetic.

Regenerated fibres These have their origin in nature, although not in the fibrous form needed for textile production. The best-known of these is viscose (also called rayon or viscose rayon) which comes from the cellulose material in wood. The trade name Durafil often describes viscose when it is used in upholstery fabric. All regenerated fabrics should be sponged carefully since they lose strength when wet.

Synthetic fibres Chemically produced, these substances originate from raw materials such as oil and coal.

Nylon One of the first synthetics produced, nylon is lightweight and very strong; it is also resistant to staining because it does not absorb moisture readily, but looks and feels unpleasant.

Acrylic Known as Courtelle, Acrilan, Orlon or Dralon (a fibre which is often woven into a fabric resembling velvet), acrylic is strong, stain-resistant and easy to look after. Often blended with wool, this material does not matt easily and retains its shape well.

Modacrylic Like acrylics, these fibres — sometimes known as Teklan or Dynel — are similar to wool in appearance and texture and often blended with wool.

The care of upholstery

Preventing wear and tear

All fabrics suffer to a greater or lesser extent from exposure to sunlight, either because it weakens the fibres or fades the colours, or both. There is no material which can withstand being in bright sunlight (especially when it is magnified by glass) all day over a long period of time, so try to position furniture out of the direct rays of the sun. Dirt also damages fibres, so clean all fabrics regularly, either with a proprietary cleaner or with a brush or vacuum cleaner as described below.

Try to keep children and animals from abusing your furniture, since they can shorten its life by many years. Bouncing will ruin springs; buckles and buttons may catch the cloth (as will animal claws); and rubber or plastic soles on shoes will quickly wear through it. Extra back and arm covers are very useful on chairs and sofas since they protect the most vulnerable areas from heavy wear. Restrict the use of aerosols such as polishes, air fresheners and insect sprays as much as possible, as these too can damage fibres.

Cleaning upholstery

Try to make a habit of vacuuming your upholstery regularly, since if you spring-clean it only once a year the dirt will become embedded in the fabric, making it very difficult to remove as well as damaging the fibres. Most suction cleaners have a special attachment for cleaning upholstery and for removing dust and dirt from awkward places in the backs and sides of chairs.

If possible, you should remove any spillage immediately after it happens. Treatment will depend on the type of fabric, so before you begin always check the manufacturer's instructions to make sure the cleaner you have in mind is suitable. You should test for such things as shrinkage and colour-fastness by experimenting with the cleaner in an inconspicuous place on the upholstery. To avoid over-dampening the fabric and the padding beneath, it is best to use a dry-cleaner to get rid of spots and stains. This type of cleaner only wets the surface and dries very quickly to a powder; when you brush off the powder, it should take the stain with it. At least one make of this type is suitable for cleaning both upholstery and carpets. Dirty marks can often be removed from fabric if you rub them with a piece of white bread.

Very badly soiled areas can be cleaned by using a special upholstery shampoo. Again, to avoid over-dampening the fabric, you can use a dry shampoo with an applicator. The shampoo foam is forced through a sponge head in a controlled flow which eventually dries to a powder and is then removed with an upholstery attachment on a vacuum cleaner. To make sure the shampoo will not harm the fabric, test it on a small, hidden area first.

Alternatively, if you are going to spring-clean your carpets by hiring a hot-water soil-extraction machine, you can clean your upholstery at the same time. Ask for a special upholstery tool attachment when you are hiring one of these machines, which are available by the day or half-day from specialist hire shops and some carpet retailers. These machines are fairly heavy to manoeuvre, but this should not be a problem when you are cleaning upholstery, since you will probably be able to reach several chairs from one position. A shampoo is mixed with hot water, 'vacuumed' over the upholstery with one sweep and sucked back with the grime and dirt in the next sweep, which takes out most of the moisture. It is best to treat very dirty areas with a spot remover to loosen the stain before using the machine. The upholstery will dry out fairly quickly in a warm room.

Repairing upholstery

A tiny tear or hole can eventually lead to a major recovering job, so it is a good idea to give your furniture a quick examination from time to time in order to catch any small accidents before they get out of control.

Tears

Burst or frayed seams and tears near piping can be repaired by slip-stitching which, if done with care, will conceal the damage. Neaten any frayed edges by trimming, but do not cut into the fabric. If necessary, turn under a tiny piece along the torn edges to neaten them. Use large darning needles fixed down firmly into the padding along the torn edges, to hold them together while slip-stitching the tear (see figure 1).

You will need matching strong thread and an upholsterer's half-circle needle. Knot one end of the thread and insert the needle into one side of the tear a little way in from the end, hiding the knot on the underside of the upholstery. Bring the two edges together by using very tiny stitches on either side, pulling the thread through very firmly each time and keeping the stitches parallel (**1**). Remove the darning needles as you go and finish by fastening off the thread, working the thread end into the seam.

Figure 1

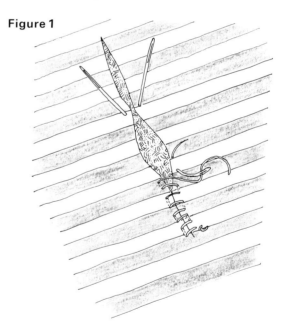

Patches

A hole can be successfully repaired by taking replacement fabric from elsewhere (the underside of the chair or sofa, for example) to use as a patch. If this is not possible and you feel it is worth the effort, try locating a piece of matching fabric from the manufacturer. Carefully cut away all the damaged fabric, tidying up the edges as you cut. The replacement patch should be slightly larger than the hole size and match any pattern on the fabric. If there is a pile make sure it runs in the same direction.

Push the patch down into position on the padding, underneath the hole edges (**2**) Coat the edges of the patch and the undersides of the fabric edges round the hole with a fabric adhesive, taking care not to let the adhesive touch anywhere else. Hold the two pieces apart for the few seconds it takes for the adhesive to become tacky, press the two surfaces together and leave them to dry. This type of patch will satisfactorily disguise small damaged areas. For anything larger you will need to fit a replacement cover for that particular section.

Figure 2

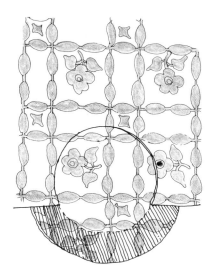

Leather and vinyl

Covers made from leather and vinyl cannot be slip-stitched, but if the material is soft, either by nature or through wear, you can repair holes and tears with a special repair kit available from most hardware stores. This kit enables you to match not only the colour but also the grain, which is particularly important if you want an inconspicuous repair.

Clean the surface with white spirit to remove grease and dirt and insert a small piece of bonding sheet (provided with the kit) through the tear to form the base for the repair paste. Mix the paste to the exact colour and use a knife or spatula to spread it on to the area. To match the grain, use one of the patterns provided with the kit; alternatively, if the grain pattern is an unusual one, you can use the rubber compound (also supplied) to make a mould of an area identical to that which is damaged, to provide a pattern. Place the grain pattern or rubber mould face down over the paste, put a piece of card on top and press down on it for two minutes with a warm iron to imprint the pattern on the paste.

Renewing and recovering a buttoned back

If you have an old chair or sofa needing some attention but which is basically in good condition, you can usually improve its appearance by renewing the buttoning, so that it looks deeper and plumper, without actually repadding the whole back. This, along with the addition of an attractive cover, will give it a new lease of life. Upholstery buttoning, however, requires some experience and should be attempted only after you have mastered some of the simpler projects (1–5) in this book.

Tools and materials

mallet
ripping chisel
tape-measure
double bayonet needle
regulator needle
slipping needle
linter felt (see figure 1)
covering fabric (see figure 2)
buttons (see project 7, figures 51–55)
twine
slipping thread
pieces of hessian — one for each button (see figure 3)
13 mm ($\frac{1}{2}$ in) fine tacks

The sofa before and after rebuttoning.

Figures 1 & 2 Preparing the covering fabric

With a mallet and chisel, carefully remove the old cover, then stretch the calico underneath taut, making a smooth surface to work on. Poke your fingers into each hole, making them as deep as possible, since the deeper the holes are the better the pleats will be between them.

Cover the back with two layers of linter felt long enough to reach from the front of one arm to the front of the other, and to tuck down between the back and the seat. The first layer should reach just to the outside edge of the top roll, and the second layer should be larger than this so that it can be tacked to the back face of the top back rail (**1**). Poke through the holes with your fingers after you have added each layer.

Figure 1

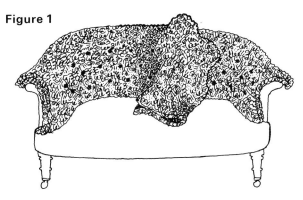

To determine how many widths of covering fabric you need, measure from the outside front edge of one arm at the widest part, in and out of each button, until you come to a measurement near to that of the fabric width — usually 122 cm (48 in). Now go back to the previous button diagonally and measure from here until you reach the width of your fabric again. Repeat until you get to the outer edge of the other arm. Now count up the total number of widths needed.

Figure 2

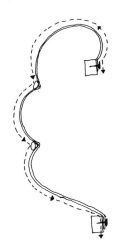

To find the length of each piece of covering fabric, measure from the bottom of the top back rail, over the back, into each hole, then down through between the back and the seat to the top of the back face of the lower back rail (**2**).

Mark out the first piece of fabric for buttoning as described in project 7, figures 51–55. Lay it in position at one arm, making sure you have enough material to pleat round the front face of the arm and to tack to the outer face of the bottom rail.

Figures 3–8 Attaching the first fabric width

Begin with the first button of the bottom row at the front of the arm. Push the fabric down into the bottom of the hole with your finger, making sure you do not take up any of the fabric which will go over the front of the arm or down between the arm and the seat.

Cut a piece of twine about three times as long as your button-holes are deep. (Our stuffing is 150 mm (6 in) thick, so each thread was cut 450 mm (18 in) long.) You will need this length of twine for each button. Thread a button on to it, then double the twine, hold the two ends together and thread them through a 150 mm (18 in) double bayonet needle.

Now insert the needle into its hole (**3**) and attach the button as explained in project 7, figures 57–58. Finish off the button completely, tying the twine on the webbing with a piece of hessian in the knot as shown in figure 6.

Figure 3

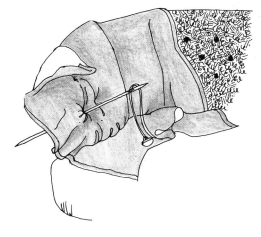

Repeat for all the buttons along the bottom row on this first piece of fabric except for the last button, leaving enough loose fabric to reach from the bottom of one hole, down into the bottom of the adjoining hole (**4**).

Figure 4

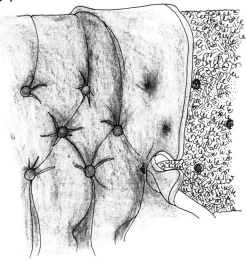

Attach the middle row of buttons, then the top row, in the same way.

Using the flat blade of a regulator, arrange the vertical pleats from the bottom row of buttons to the seat, pushing the fabric between the seat and the back and cutting into the fabric carefully at the inside corner so that it can be pushed down at both sides of the back rail (**5**). From the outside, pull both pieces of fabric through and, with your regulator, arrange the bottom row of vertical pleats again. Insert temporary tacks into the rail at the base of each pleat (**6**). When all the pleats have been done, check to make sure they are as even as possible, then drive the tacks home.

Figure 5

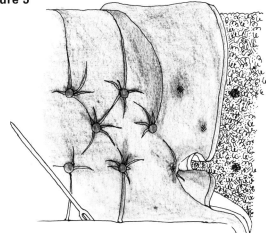

At the front of the arm, cut into the fabric at the inside towards the back of the front arm rail. Pull the fabric down behind the front arm rail. Trim. Pull the front edge of the fabric over the front of

Figure 6

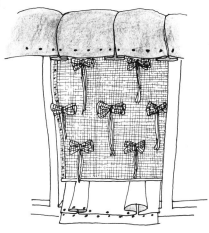

the arm, towards the outside (**7**), so that its edge is parallel to the vertical edge of the front rail, and anchor it at the lowest point with a temporary tack, making sure the horizontal grain of the fabric is parallel with the seat.

Figure 7

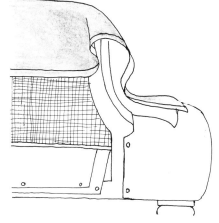

Pull the top edge of the fabric over the curve of the arm towards the outside, making the fabric as smooth and tight as possible. Temporarily tack it to the outer face of the front arm rail. Pull the rest of the front edge of fabric to the front of the chair in the same way and temporarily tack it here. It will probably be necessary to do a lot of pulling, rearranging and retacking for a

Figure 8

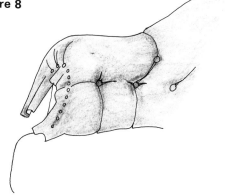

satisfactory result and no buttoning over a curved, traditionally padded surface will ever be perfect.

When you have done the best you can, drive home the temporary tacks along the outside rails.

Release the temporary tacks at the front of the arm, cut off any excess fabric, arrange the fullness into even pleats and tack these permanently to the front of the arm (**8**).

Figures 9-11 Finishing the arm front panel

Cut a rectangle of fabric large enough to cover the arm front generously. Lay it over the inside of the arm, right sides together (see figure 9), with one edge of it over the inside of the arm front. Tack down a strip of back tacking (or stiff card) over this fabric edge from the bottom of the front of the arm up as far as you can go without going round the outside of the curve (**9**).

Figure 9

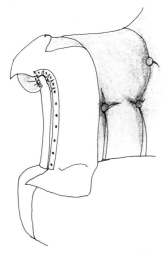

Pull the fabric over towards the outside arm and insert a piece of Courtelle (or linter felt) slightly wider than this piece of fabric to make a lightly padded curve (**10**). Fold the fabric under to make a neat edge at the bottom. Turn under a

Figure 10

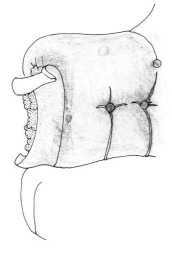

small hem at the top and, with a slipping needle, slip-stitch the fabric around the curve with tiny stitches (**11**).

Figure 11

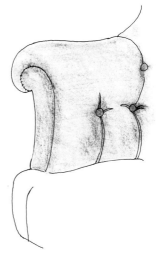

Figures 12-14 The second fabric width

At the other, buttoned end of your fabric width, cut a V-shape as shown, leaving at least 25 mm (1 in) beyond each last button-hole.

Line up the top edge of your next fabric width (marked as before) with the existing fabric. Lay the new width on the first width, overlapping the next holes to be buttoned by at least 25 mm (1 in). Cut a V-shape parallel to the V-shape in the first width.

Thread a button on to the needle and, beginning with the central button-hole, insert the point of your needle through the two layers of fabric at the point of the V-shape (**12**). (Hold the first width of fabric in place with your fingers so it will be caught in the point of the needle.)

Figure 12

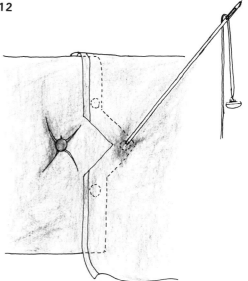

Care, repairs and finishing

Attach the button in the usual way. Before you finish the join, you should attach a few more buttons so the fabric is secure; to do this, first attach the next button in the middle row, then the one in the top row, above and between the two you have just attached, then the equivalent one in the bottom row (**13**).

Figure 13

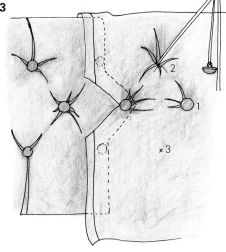

Now go back to where the widths are being joined, at the top row of buttons. Again anchoring the first width with your finger, pull the new width into position with your other hand so it fits tightly over the stuffing and into the hole. When you are holding the two layers securely together, put your needle through them and attach the button as before. The pleat formed should face down.

Attach the nearest button to the join in the bottom row in the same way. Ideally, all the pleats going between the buttons should face down toward the seat, but this one will face up (**14**). This is not very important with most fabrics and it should not show, but if it does, and you are worried about it, make a tiny cut very carefully just above the lowest button,

Figure 14

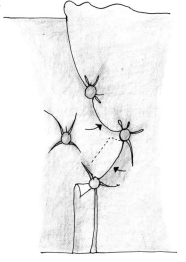

so that you can lift the first width up and put it down over the second one. This is a very tricky process and can easily cause the fabric to tear, so do not take it on unless you really must.

Continue buttoning and joining widths as described until you reach the other arm. Finish this in exactly the same way as you did the first. Now tack down along the back, arranging the pleats as you did at the bottom (see figure 5). Finish off according to the appropriate instructions in the earlier projects.

Making a tailored skirt

A tailored skirt with box pleats at the corners is simple to make and attach round the bottom of an upholstered chair or sofa.

Tools and materials

pins
string
tape-measure
scissors
covering fabric to match the rest of the chair, as wide as the height the skirt will be and 1110 mm (44 in) longer than the perimeter of the chair, plus bias strips for piping
lining fabric the same length and 13 mm ($\frac{1}{2}$ in) narrower than the covering fabric
piping cord the length of the perimeter of the seat plus 50 mm (2 in)
slipping needle and thread

A tailored skirt with corner pleats gives an attractive finish to any chair or sofa.

Figures 1-5 Making up

With a pin, mark on one corner of the chair the point where you want the top of the skirt to be. Measure its distance from the floor on the other three corners. Join up these four pins with a length of string running all round the chair. This will give you a guide for attaching the finished skirt, and an indication of the width of fabric needed. (Since there will be a 13 mm ($\frac{1}{2}$ in) seam allowance, the finished skirt will clear the floor by this amount.)

Cut out four strips of fabric as wide as the height of the skirt, each one the length of one of the four sides of the chair, plus 90 mm ($3\frac{1}{2}$ in).

Now cut four extra pieces of fabric to the same width, but 190 mm ($7\frac{1}{2}$ in) long; these will form the insides of the pleats. With right sides together and allowing 13 mm ($\frac{1}{2}$ in) for seams, stitch all the pieces end to end in a continuous band, each long one in the sequence in which it will fall round the chair.

Make up a circle of lining fabric to the same length but 13 mm ($\frac{1}{2}$ in) narrower – it does not matter where the joins fall. Sew this to the right side of your fabric strip, edge to edge, again leaving a 13 mm ($\frac{1}{2}$ in) seam allowance. Turn the skirt right side out and press it so that the two free raw edges meet. This will ensure that the lining is well concealed behind the skirt.

Pin the skirt temporarily into place on the chair with the lining side out, raw edges at the top and the centre of each short piece falling at each corner. Attach it so that it fits tightly round the chair except for a large loop of fabric at each corner. Pin the loops in position at the top at each corner (**1**).

Figure 1

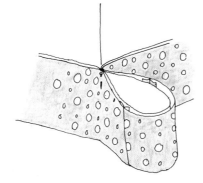

Take the skirt off the chair and sew each loop down at the point where you pinned it to 50 mm (2 in) from the top edge (**2**). Now press and pin the loop flat so that there are equal amounts of fabric at each side of the vertical seam, forming a pleat (**3**).

Figure 2

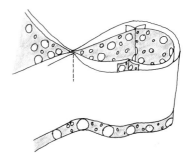

Figure 3

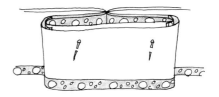

Pin a length of piping to the top of the skirt, right sides and all raw edges together. (Instructions for making piping are given in project 1, figures 21–25.) Sew the piping to the skirt, stitching straight across the pleats at the corners (**4**). Neaten the ends and press so that the seam allowances are tucked down behind the piping.

Figure 4

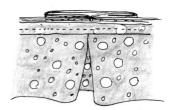

Ease the finished skirt (**5**) back into position on the chair from below, pin and slip-stitch it to the cover

Figure 5

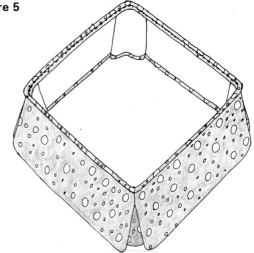

Index

Further reading

BARBARA JONES *English Furniture at a Glance* (Architectural Press, London 1954)

JANET LILLY *Know About Furniture* (Blackie, Glasgow 1976)

MOLLY HARRISON *People and Furniture* (Benn, London 1971)

EDWARD T. JOY *Country Life Book of Chairs* (Country Life Books, London 1967)

RAY WATKINSON *William Morris as Designer* (Studio Vista, London 1967)

ERIC MERCER *Furniture 700–1700* (Weidenfeld & Nicolson, London 1969)

DUNJA JOGAN

FELIX
AFTER
THE RAIN

TINY OWL

Felix was a terribly
unhappy boy.

He dragged an enormous
suitcase behind him
wherever he went.

But he didn't know
what was inside.

Something dark had appeared in the suitcase
when Grandma died.

Something hurtful had hidden inside
when his friends made fun of him.

Something bothersome had burrowed its way in
when his Dad told him off.

The suitcase became heavier and heavier.

Felix could barely manage to push it along.

If only he could leave it somewhere
and escape across the ocean.

But the sea was so rough
and the winds were so wild.

Grandma used to say to Felix
that the sun always shines after the rain
and that after every uphill climb
there's a downhill stroll.

One day, Felix reached the top of the hill, puffing and panting.
He lay down in the shade and fell asleep.

A small boy was playing nearby.
He caught sight of the suitcase, crept towards it and opened it up.

All of a sudden,
the sky turned grey.

Felix found himself
in the middle of a storm.

He felt a rumble in his head, and his eyes filled
with tears that ran down
his cheeks like the rain.

When the storm had settled,
Felix felt calm too.

"What did you do with
the suitcase?"
he asked the curious boy.

He just smiled,
and Felix thanked him.

Felix came down from the hilltop
and he looked at
the clouds in the sky.

He smelt the blossom on the trees and listened
to the hum of the friendly breeze.

Without a care in the world,
he leapt towards the clear blue sea.

"I feel like a fish in water!"

He returned home empty handed
but with a heart full of happiness.

It lifted him off the ground like a balloon.

Felix was so happy,
he wanted to give
everyone a hug.

And everyone gently
hugged Felix.